Celebrations!

ALL AGE WORSHIP

Celebrations!
ALL AGE WORSHIP

NICK & CLAIRE PAGE

Authentic

LONDON ● COLORADO SPRINGS ● HYDERABAD

Copyright © 2007 Nick and Claire Page

13 12 11 10 09 08 07   7 6 5 4 3 2 1

First published 2007 by Authentic Media
9 Holdom Avenue, Bletchley, Milton Keynes, Bucks, MK1 1QR, UK

1820 Jet Stream Drive, Colorado Springs, CO 80921, USA

OM Authentic Media, Medchal Road, Jeedimetla Village,
Secunderabad 500 055, A.P., India

www.authenticmedia.co.uk

Authentic Media is a division of IBS-STL UK, a company limited by guarantee (registered charity no. 270162)

British Library Cataloguing in Publication Data

A catalogue record for this book is available from the British Library

ISBN-13: 978-1-85078-746-4

ISBN-10: 1-85078-746-8

Unless otherwise stated all Scripture quotations are from the
Contemporary English Version, Copyright © 1995 by American Bible Society. Used by permission.

Book Design by Nick Page

Cover Design by fourninezero design.

Print Management by Adare

Printed and bound in Great Britain by J. Haynes & Co., Sparkford.

Contents

Read this first

'You know you're doing the service on Sunday? Well I forgot to tell you – it's an All Age Service.'

How would you react to those words? With a thrill in your heart and a Bambi-like skip in your step? Or would you break out into a cold sweat and develop an alarming twitch?

All Age Services can be daunting affairs – even for those who enjoy them. They need a lot of energy and inventiveness. Which is where this book comes in.

The style

The ideas in this book use action, discussion and entertainment. We make no apology for this. Research has shown that sitting still and listening is possibly the least effective way of learning. Done well, services that involve movement and activity, listening and watching, problem-solving and reflection, can be hugely effective. Give people something to do – a problem to solve, a place to go to – and they become part of the teaching themselves.[1] You shouldn't come to church just to sit still, either literally or spiritually.

Following the script

This book is designed for whole-service teaching. Every part of the service is designed to move the 'lesson' forward. A lot of the book is in a script format, but that doesn't mean you have to act it and be all dramatic! It just indicates who says what, and when. It's no different to liturgy – which is, essentially, a scripted service. And although we are aiming to involve the children in the teaching, this approach could be used for adults-only services just as well. Why should they miss out on all the fun?

Using the ideas

You can use this book in the following ways:

▷ Do the services exactly as they are presented. From beginning to end.

▷ Pick which bits of the services work for you and use those.

▷ Nick the ideas and adapt them to your own ends!

Up to you

These services are the basis for improvisation. Jazz chords, not Bach fugues. You can go where you like with them, add in what you like, leave out what you wish, use all of it, use most of it, use some of it, use hardly any of it, use just the tiniest nano-section of it, use... well, you get the point.

Anyway, if you break into a cold sweat the next time someone says, 'Oh, by the way, it's an All Age Service', you can't blame us!

---

1 A lot of our approach is based on the Accelerated Learning techniques. We'd recommend the book to anyone involved in teaching: Dave Meier, *The Accelerated Learning Handbook* (New York: McGraw-Hill, 2000).

Overview

The first two pages give an overview of the service, showing the overall aim and how the whole thing fits together. Each service is split into four parts:

1. Want It!

This is where you introduce the subject matter and get people interested in learning. To teach people properly, you have to make them curious and interested enough to learn. Ice-breakers set the tone of the service; the introduction is a promise of what they're going to get.

2. Watch It!

This is the place for the Bible readings or sketches or presentations. Although people watch this bit, they don't sit still. Discussions, treasure hunts, acting scenes out; there's a lot of moving around and discovery.

3. Try It!

This is where they learn for themselves: reflecting, praying, solving problems. The golden rule of teaching is: don't spoon feed your students. Teach them what they need to know, then get out the way as quick as you can!

4. Live It!

This is where you help people to take the learning forward into the coming week: something to take away as a reminder or as a stimulus to action, or a challenge to face up to – applying Sunday teaching to Monday-to-Friday lives.

Running order

This is a simple grid which can be photocopied, listing the elements of the service. You can add in your own details, such as hymns/songs, notices, timings, etc. You can also fill in the initials of whoever is responsible for any of this.

Resources

The next few pages give the actual resources for the service: games, drama, discussions, prayers and more. These are grouped under the Want it! Watch it! Try it! Live it! headings.

Talks

We have kept the direct talk to the congregation to a minimum. It's a sermon-free zone. There are sections for 'the Leader' to say. You are, of course, free to add in whatever you want. You can use the DIY boxes *(see right)* to put the main points in your own words. Or you can say exactly what you want.

DIY

▷If you want to stray off the text or put things in your own words, the DIY boxes summarise the main speech in a few bullet points.

Discussion

 ▷ Questions in these boxes are discussion points. This is where you get the congregation to do some of the work.

Ensure the questions are clear and that there is enough time for people to have a go. Get feedback whenever possible – but vary the ways you do it. And keep it short.

Creating groups

Every service makes use of group work. Sometimes it's best – as is suggested by PairTalk – simply to turn to the person nearby. When larger groups are called for, you can try different ways of creating a mix of people such as grouping people according to which month they were born in, what their first name or surname begins with, height order, or simply numbering them off, if the congregation isn't too numerous. Not everybody wants to be co-erced into groupwork, so it takes a bit of tact and charm to persuade people. But it's worth the effort!

Moving stories

Several of the Bible passages are illustrated with a lot of movement. These moving stories are ways of acting out the Bible passage rather than just having to sit and listen to them. The more people who can move, the better.

Drama

There's a lot of drama in these services. Some sketches need to be learnt, but most dialogue can be read off the page.

Recurring characters

The Shy Spies

The Shy Spies are a classic double act and can easily be improvised once you've grasped the basic facts about them. These two characters 'investigate' the Bible passage, getting the congregation to collect and interpret clues. We've scripted some lines, but the discussion parts are up to you.

▷ Each Spy wears a raincoat with the collar up, shades and a trilby.

▷ Agent X is generally cleverer than Y, who is ready to believe anything, and needs things explaining.

▷ They act as if permanently under surveillance, looking around them for bugs, and talking – at least at the start – in a loud whisper.

▷ The first time you introduce these characters you can use the introductory script on p.124.

Gordon the Gargoyle

Gordon the Gargoyle helps us apply what we've learned. We attend an Anglican Church where, high up inside the building, there are a number of carved stone heads. One of those became Gordon, who has been in the church for centuries and seen it all. Gordon was voiced by Nick (hiding in a side room with a microphone). Of course your church might not have gargoyles, internal or otherwise. You have a number of choices here.

▷ Build your own gargoyle and tell people you thought that all churches should have one.

▷ Turn Gordon into another character. There are a lot of puns using rock, stone, etc. so he could be a statue, or some part of the building. He could simply be a rock, called Rocky. Or Barney the Brick.

▷ You could use a puppet – perhaps a kind of grandfather character. Just use the scripts and adapt them to your purpose.

We realise this isn't ideal, but we couldn't bear to leave him out! The first time you introduce Gordon you can use the introductory script on p.125.

TakeAway

This is something for the participants to take away with them from the service, to remind them of something they've decided to do.

Extras

Getting ready

A checklist of jobs that need to be done during the week before, or on the morning of the service.

Might come in handy

Contains some interesting facts or background material that you can use in your talks or links, should you want to.

Know your audience

Aside from having a good programme, one of the most important factors in the success of All-Age services – or, indeed, any communication – is to know your audience. If you have a good relationship with the people in your congregation and know them well enough, you will be able to adapt the programme to suit your particular circumstances. So take a careful look at the distribution of ages, the gender mix and the ability spectrum. In particular we need to think about

▷ people who are deaf or who have partial hearing

▷ the blind or partially sighted

▷ those with restricted mobility

▷ anyone with cognitive learning difficulties (mild, moderate or profound)[2]

2 For help in thinking about their needs, and useful approaches to consider, see *Access for all* available from: The Basic Skills Agency, Admail 524, London WC1A 1BR.

New Year

1. NEW YEAR

Title: Wise up!
Aim: To ask for God's wisdom
Bible: 1 Kings 3.5–15, 16–22, 23–28

1. Want It!

The purpose here is to
▷ make people keen to be wise

We do this by asking people to
▷ make three wishes and imagine the outcome
▷ evaluate the wisdom of their decision

The tools we use are
▷ Introduction: New Year's resolutions
▷ PairTalk: my three wishes

2. Watch It!

The purpose here is to
▷ notice what King Solomon wished for and why

We do this by asking people to
▷ watch or take part in the drama
▷ list the benefits of wisdom

The tools we use are
▷ Bible: I Kings 3.5–15: Solomon's wish
▷ The Shy Spies investigate: the benefits of wisdom

3. Try It!

The purpose here is to
▷ pray for wisdom for ourselves and others
▷ test our ability to make wise decisions

We do this by asking people to
▷ pray for national leaders
▷ solve problems in groups

The tools we use are
▷ Dilemma: the baby with two mums
▷ Advice to Solomon
▷ Prayers: for people who need wisdom

4. Live It!

The purpose here is to
▷ keep asking God for wisdom

We do this by asking people to
▷ listen to Gordon and leader
▷ make a memory magnet to TakeAway

The tools we use are
▷ Gordon's New Year resolution
▷ Help yourself: three steps to wisdom
▷ TakeAway: memory magnet
▷ Closing prayer

Running order

When	What	Who
	Want it!	
	Introduction: New Year's resolutions	
	PairTalk: my three wishes	
	Watch it!	
	Bible: 1 Kings 3.5–15: Solomon's wish	
	The Shy Spies investigate: the benefits of wisdom	
	Try it!	
	Dilemma: 1 Kings 3.16–28: the baby with two mums	
	Advice to Solomon	
	Prayers for people who need wisdom	
	Live it!	
	Gordon's New Year resolution	
	Help yourself: three steps to wisdom	
	TakeAway: memory magnet	
	Closing prayer	

Want it!

Introduction: New Year's resolutions

LEADER: Good morning and a happy New Year!

New Year is a great time to look back and reflect on the year that's gone, as well as looking forward to the coming year with all its hopes and opportunities.

It's traditional at this time of year to make New Year's resolutions: promises to yourself of good habits you're going to adopt, bad habits you're going to kick.

DIY

▷ Welcome and introduction

▷ Talk about New Year's resolutions

▷ Ask people to make three wishes

We're going to think about that this morning. But right now, as it's still panto season, instead of making some resolutions, I'm going to ask you to make three wishes. If a fairy godmother could appear right now and grant you three wishes, what would they be? Riches? Beauty? Long life? Discuss it with the person next to you.

▷ What would you wish for?
▷ How would life change if you had your three wishes?

PairTalk: my three wishes

LEADER: It's fun to daydream and to imagine what we would do if we were really given the chance. Many fairytales are based on this idea. There's a story like this, too, in the Bible, of one person – a king – who was given the chance to ask for anything he wanted. Let's see what he chose.

Watch it!

Bible: 1 Kings 3.5–15a: Solomon's wish

Enter King Solomon, dressed in pyjamas, with a crown on his head. He is standing up, but he has a pillow secured to the back of his head by a head band and holds a duvet vertically, so it looks like he's in bed. The Lord's voice can be amplified from off stage.

NARRATOR: One night while Solomon was in Gibeon, the Lord God appeared to him in a dream and said:

THE LORD: Solomon, ask for anything you want, and I will give it to you.

SOLOMON: My father David, your servant, was honest and did what you commanded. You were always loyal to him, and you gave him a son who is now king. LORD God, I'm your servant, and you've made me king in my father's place.

But I'm very young and know so little about being a leader. And now I must rule your chosen people, even though there are too many of them to count.

Please make me wise and teach me the difference between right and wrong. Then I will know how to rule your people. If you don't, there is no way I could rule this great nation of yours.

THE LORD: Solomon, I'm pleased that you asked for this. You could have asked to live a long time or to be rich. Or you could have asked for your enemies to be destroyed. Instead, you asked for wisdom to make right decisions. So I'll make you wiser than anyone who has ever lived or ever will live. I'll also give you what you didn't ask for. You'll be rich and respected as long as you live, and you'll be greater than any other king. If you obey me and follow my commands, as your father David did, I'll let you live a long time.

NARRATOR: Solomon woke up and realised that God had spoken to him in the dream.

The Shy Spies investigate: the benefits of wisdom

Enter the Shy Spies. If this is your first encounter with the Shy Spies you might want to use the introduction script on p.124.

X: I'm Agent X:

Y: I'm Agent Y.

X and Y: *(Together)* And we're the Shy Spies. Shhhhhhh.

X: We've come from our bosses...

Y: ...B and Q.

X and Y: *(Together)* And they've given us a mission to do.

X: We have reason to believe that there are ten clues about wisdom, hidden in this place. We need to find them and make sure these people see them. Apparently they could do with a bit of wisdom.

Y: And what's in it for us, X?

X: Well, firstly, this codebook *(holds up Bible)* says that 'Wisdom is like honey for your life. If you find it, your future is bright.'

Y: I like the sound of the money.

X: Not money. *Honey.* Anyway, we need to find this wisdom, quick. Perhaps my sonic-clue-finder will do it for us. *(Waves it around; it doesn't do anything)* Or not. *(Addressing audience)* Do you think you could find these clues? We obviously need to act as quietly as possible at all times.

The Shy Spies send the children and adults off to find clues. As the clues are found, peg them up onto a line, hang them on the Christmas tree, if you have one in your church, or simply pin them on a board. Make sure everyone can read them easily.

Clue	Teaching Point
Proverbs 8.15–16	Wisdom helps leaders to rule justly.
Proverbs 1.2–4	Wisdom gives understanding, self-control, knowledge and good sense.
Proverbs 1.32–3	Wisdom gives safety and security.
Proverbs 2.4–5	Wisdom helps you know the Lord.
Proverbs 2.9	Wisdom helps you know what's right and fair.
Proverbs 2.12	Wisdom will protect you from evil schemes.
Proverbs 3.16	Wisdom brings wealth and honour.
Proverbs 3.17	Wisdom makes life pleasant.
Proverbs 3.18	Wisdom brings happiness.
Proverbs 3.21–24	Wisdom can help you sleep soundly!
Proverbs 5.1–2	Wisdom helps you know the right thing to say.
Proverbs 9.11	Wisdom can help you live a long time.
Proverbs 12.18	Wisdom can heal broken relationships.
Proverbs 24.5	Wisdom makes you strong.

After each clue has been found and read out, ask the congregation to explain what it means. When all the clues have been found....

X: Come on Y, we've got to get back to B & Q.

Y: You mean, report back to the bosses?

X: No, I've got to get a bit of laminate flooring – the wife wants to redecorate the living room.

Spies exit

LEADER: Brilliant. You found the clues about wisdom. So can you tell me...

▷ How can wisdom help you in your daily life?
▷ Did anyone choose wisdom as one of their three wishes? Why?

Try it!

LEADER: So wisdom is a good thing. According to the Bible, it brings lots of benefits. King Solomon needed wisdom to make fair judgements. We do, too. So let's try it out. You are going to be Wise Men. And Women. Here's what you have to do: we're going to show you one of Solomon's dilemmas and you have to suggest a solution.

Dilemma: 1 Kings 3.16–22: the baby with two mums

Read it, or watch it being acted out

LEADER: One day two women presented themselves before King Solomon.

WOMAN 1: Your Majesty, this woman and I live in the same house. The other day, I gave birth to a baby boy at home, while she was there. Two days later, she also gave birth to a baby boy.

Only the two of us were there in the house. No-one else was present. Then, one night, she accidentally rolled over on her baby and smothered it!

Anyway, she got up, took my baby while I was asleep, and carried him to her bed and she put the dead child in my bed. Next morning, I wake up, I go to feed the baby, I see it's dead! Then I look more closely and, well – it's not my child!

LEADER: But the other woman said:

WOMAN 2: *(Without any emotion)* Rubbish. The living baby is mine, and the dead one is hers.

WOMAN 1: No! The dead child is yours, and the living one is mine!

LEADER: And so they argued before the king.

Advice to Solomon

▷ What would you advise the king to do?
▷ Can you think of other situations where you need wisdom?

Encourage feedback. If no-one's suggested it, show what happened.

LEADER: So we can see that Solomon was very wise to ask for wisdom!

Prayers for wisdom

LEADER: It's good to talk about our wishes with God in prayer. In the story today we heard God ask Solomon: What would you like me to give you?

However, prayer is not just about asking God to make our wishes come true. He is our Father and Teacher as well.

Psalm 37.4 tells us 'Delight yourself in the Lord and he will give you the desires of your heart.'

As we come to love him and his ways, we will want what he wants and, in the process, will become wise about our wishes. He may well give us the 'desires of our heart' – but he may want us to learn something about ourselves or others, or him, along the way. So let's pray.

DIY

▷It is good to share our wishes with God

▷But God is not some kind of 'fairy-godmother'

▷He wants us to learn about him as well

Prayer for wisdom for ourselves

Lord, let me tell you the things I'd really like.

(Long silence)

Now, I will listen to you. What would you really like for me?

(Long silence)

Amazing Father, God of our Lord Jesus Christ, give me your wise and holy Spirit.

Help me to understand what it means to know you.

Thank you for work and play, and all that you've given me to do.

Please give me the knowledge and wisdom I need to do it well.

Inspire me, so that I live for you, and so have joy and peace.

Amen

Prayer for people making difficult decisions

Suggest that people pray for one another, without necessarily sharing the details. You can have the following sample prayer ready for people to use if they want.

Lord, today I pray for ... sitting next to me, who needs your wisdom.

Please help ... to listen to you, to hear your voice, and to follow your wisdom as he/she makes decisions this week, and this year.

Amen

Prayers for powerful people

LEADER: Let us pray for our leaders and for all those who make important decisions.

We ask that they would draw close to you

ALL: And stay by your side

LEADER: To seek your golden wisdom

ALL: Not riches or long life

LEADER: To rule your people justly

ALL: Not with revenge or spite

LEADER: But to know the difference between good and evil.

Wisdom begins with respect for the Lord.

ALL: Lord give our leaders wisdom. Give our leaders life.

Amen

Live it!

Gordon's New Year Resolution

If this is your first meeting with Gordon you might want to use the introduction script on p.125.

LEADER: So, New Year is a time for making resolutions. I wonder if there's anyone here who made a resolution before coming here?

GORDON: Hello! Hello!

LEADER: Hello, Gordon! How are you? Did you have a good New Year?

GORDON: Yes, thank you. All of us gargoyles watched our favourite film.

LEADER: What's that?

GORDON: *Rocky*.

LEADER: What about New Year's resolutions? Have you made any?

GORDON: Well, each year I resolve not to make any New Year's resolutions. But I always fail.

LEADER: So you *do* make resolutions.

GORDON: Yes, this year I'm a bit overweight. I need to lose a stone. Then I'll be virtually perfect.

LEADER: Very modest, aren't you?

GORDON: It's funny you should say that, because I've resolved not to be so modest in future. I tend to hide my light under a bushel. I'll have to be a bit of a bolder boulder. I've also resolved to stay awake during ... 's sermons. *(Use the name of a preacher in your church who won't be offended!)* 'Cos he gets quite lonely standing up there talking to himself.

LEADER: Anything else?

GORDON: Well, I'm going to change my appearance so I'm more like my hero.

LEADER: Who's that?

GORDON: Cliff.

LEADER: Have you thought about trying to be more wise? That's what we've been talking about today – trying to be wise. Where did you get your wisdom from?

GORDON: I got it from my Dad. Even though he was carved in the reign of William the Conqueror, he's very wise.

LEADER: Is he?

GORDON: Yes. It's what's called Norman Wisdom.

LEADER: Right. Well, let's hope the jokes are going to get better in the next year, eh?

Help yourself: three steps to wisdom

DIY

> ▷Ultimately wisdom comes from God
>
> ▷Three ways to wise up
>
> Ask God for wisdom (Prov. 3.5–6)
>
> Seek advice from others (Prov. 3.10)
>
> Make friends with wise people (Prov. 13.20)
>
> ▷Introduce memory magnet

LEADER: Gordon's really like the rest of us. Ultimately we all get wisdom from our father – not necessarily our Dads here on earth – although I'm sure they're wise – but from our Heavenly Father. That's who gave Solomon his wisdom and he still wants to help us today.

So how are you going to wise up this year? As we've seen, the Bible tells us what we need to do to become wise. If you want to get more wisdom into your life this year, here are three things you can do.

1. Ask God for wisdom – like Solomon

Wisdom comes from God. So that's where we start. Pray to God to give you more wisdom. He wants to help (Prov. 3.5–6).

2. Don't be scared to ask for advice – from parents and others

If you've got to make difficult decisions, ask for advice. Believe it or not, a lot of parents are wiser than you think (Prov. 13.1).

3. Make friends with wise people

Wisdom is catching! The more time you spend with wise people, the more you will learn from them. But watch out: the Bible also warns us about spending time with foolish people. You can catch stupidity as well (Prov. 13.20)!

TakeAway: a memory magnet

Provide each person with a strip of magnetic paper and a pen.

LEADER: It's hard trying to keep New Year's resolutions, as we heard from Gordon. How are you going to make this one stick? Choose one of the proverbs you've heard today and rewrite it in your own words as your resolution on the magnet. You can put it up when you get home. Perhaps on the mirror or the fridge.

Closing prayer

You could teach this prayer, asking people to copy you, line by line.

Lord, in the year that's about to start,
Help me to love you with all my heart.
Help me to listen: I want to be wise.
Help me to see the world through your eyes.
Amen

Might come in handy

About King Solomon

According to Chronicles, his name indicates that during his reign, the Lord would keep Israel quiet and peaceful (1 Chr. 22.9).

He was David's tenth son. His mother was Bathsheba, and he ruled Israel from around 960 to 922bc.

God's appearance to Solomon in a dream showed that God was prepared to do great things for Solomon and his people. And, in many ways, Solomon's reign was a golden age for Israel. He expanded the city of Jerusalem and built the Temple to house the Ark of the Covenant. He 'excelled all the kings of the earth in riches and in wisdom' (2 Chr. 9.22). He wrote psalms and collected proverbs, and even became an expert on botany and zoology (1Kgs. 4.32–33).

He had a famous meeting with the Queen of Sheba who, after observing his wealth and wisdom, showered him with gifts.

At the same time, his tax-raising policies and use of forced labour from other tribes aroused great resentment and contributed to the split of the kingdoms after his death (1Kgs. 12.1–15).

Most surprisingly, Solomon ended his life as a worshipper of false gods and idols. He married hundreds of wives (including the daughter of the Pharaoh of Egypt) and had many concubines, and their influence lured him away from worshipping the true God (1Kgs. 11.1–13).

About Gibeon

Six miles north west of Jerusalem, before the Temple was built, Gibeon was home to one of the most important shrines in Israel.

Both the Tabernacle and the Ark of the Covenant spent time there during David's reign (1 Chr. 16.39; 21.29; 2 Chr. 1.3,13). It was important, therefore, that Solomon should make a sacrifice there at the start of his reign.

The sacrifice was attended by all of Solomon's leadership team and some thousand offerings were burnt, showing what an important state occasion it was.

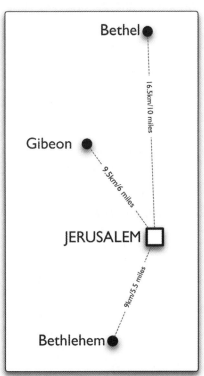

Getting ready

A week (or more) before

Questions

☐ Put questions on Power-point or notice sheet

Solomon's wish

☐ Copy scripts and give out parts to actors

☐ Rehearse drama

☐ Gather any props/costumes/set

Shy Spies

☐ Gather props and costumes: coats, hats, shades, sonic clue-finder

☐ Allocate parts of X, Y, distribute scripts

☐ Print clues

☐ Find way to display clues

Dilemmas and problem-solving

☐ Print out scripts and allocate parts or print out scenario

Gordon's New Year resolution

☐ Copy script

Help yourself

☐ Put Bible verses onto Power-point or notice sheet

TakeAway

☐ Buy magnetic paper and cut up into 'fridge magnet' size lengths

☐ Gather biros or marker pens to write on magnetic paper

An hour (or more) before

Solomon's wish

☐ Arrange seating and set throne for Solomon

☐ Put props and costumes in place

Gordon's New Year resolution

☐ Set-up for Gordon (microphone, statue, etc. as required)

Shy Spies

☐ Put props, costumes and clues in place

TakeAway

☐ Put resources in place

Celebrations!

Palm
Sunday

2. PALM SUNDAY

Title: And the crowd are going wild!
Aim: To go wild about Jesus!
Bible: John 12.12–19; other gospel accounts

1. Want It!

The purpose here is to

▷ get people to identify how reserved or excitable they are normally

▷ ask what they find exciting about Jesus

We do this by asking people to

▷ play a game

▷ talk to each other in pairs

The tools we use are

▷ Game: the stiff upper lip game

▷ PairTalk: why is Jesus so exciting?

2. Watch It!

The purpose here is to

▷ picture the scene on Palm Sunday

▷ imagine how Lazarus was feeling

We do this by asking people to

▷ listen to the Bible

▷ search for clues

The tools we use are

▷ Bible: John 12.12–19

▷ The Shy Spies investigate: the Lazarus trail

3. Try It!

The purpose here is to

▷ help people relive the story

▷ express praise and worship, both with noise and silence

We do this by asking people to

▷ take part in a procession

▷ meditate on a Bible verse

The tools we use are

▷ A moving story: Palm Sunday procession

▷ Meditation: stony silence

4. Live It!

The purpose here is to

▷ help people live with a fresh sense of excitement about Jesus

We do this by asking people to

▷ listen to Gordon

▷ write a verse of praise on bandages or stones

The tools we use are

▷ Gordon gets excited

▷ TakeAway: a stone

▷ Closing prayer

Running order

When	What	Who
	Want it!	
	The stiff upper lip game	
	PairTalk: why is Jesus so exciting?	
	Watch it!	
	Bible: John 12.12–19	
	The Shy Spies investigate: the Lazarus trail	
	Try it!	
	A moving story: Palm Sunday procession	
	Meditation: stony silence	
	Live it!	
	Gordon gets excited	
	TakeAway: a stone	
	Closing prayer	

Want it!

The stiff upper lip game

LEADER: Are you naturally quiet and reserved or are you loud and lairy? How often do you get really excited and let it all hang out?

For the following game choose a few questions, then ask people to respond in one of the following ways: either

▷ Answer 'Yes' by moving to one wall or 'No' by going to the opposite wall. You'll soon find out how reserved your church is!

▷ Or you could ask them just to use their hands, to put palms up for a 'Yes' and palms down for a 'No.'

LEADER: We're a mix of characters – some wildly enthusiastic, some terribly British and reserved. Today we're going to be hearing about a crowd that really went wild, cheering Jesus on the day when he entered Jerusalem.

▷ Do you leap up out of bed in the morning?
▷ Do you dream of being a famous movie star?
▷ Do you like being hugged?
▷ When you sing in church, do you feel like you want to dance as well?
▷ Do you sing in the bath?
▷ When you are in a crowd at a sports event, do you shout for your team?
▷ Have you ever screamed at a concert (at a pop star)?
▷ Do you sing the national anthem on Remembrance Sunday?
▷ Have you ever cheered for a member of the Royal Family?
▷ Have you ever taken part in a protest march?
▷ Do you like audience participation/ interactive stuff/getting up and doing things in a church service?

Read Luke 19.38–40

LEADER: I wonder why they were so excited about Jesus? Who did they think he was?

Feedback from congregation – ask for different titles of Jesus.

He is described in the Bible in many different ways

▷ The Messiah
▷ The Christ
▷ The King
▷ Saviour

▷ Redeemer
▷ The Word of God
▷ The Good Shepherd
▷ Master
▷ Teacher
▷ The great High Priest

▷	The Son of God	▷	King of Kings
▷	The Son of Man	▷	Prince of Peace
▷	The Holy One of God	▷	Son of David
▷	Lord	▷	Immanuel
▷	Lord of Lords	▷	The Lamb of God
▷	King of Israel	▷	The Alpha and the Omega

LEADER: Imagine someone like that riding into town. Wouldn't you be excited?

PairTalk – Why is Jesus exciting?

▷ Which description do you like the best?
▷ Can you think of a time when you got so excited about Jesus, you just had to tell someone about him? What did you say?

Watch it!

LEADER: So we have seen that there was a big procession. But I wonder who was there?

▷ Who do you think was in that procession?

LEADER: One person we think was there was a man called Lazarus. It would be good to hear from him, if we can. Let's see if the Shy Spies can help.

The Shy Spies investigate: the Lazarus trail

The Shy Spies enter, as usual, as if they are looking for someone. They are hiding behind their newspapers and are trying to look inconspicuous. They have been spying on the crowd, following Jesus' entry to Jerusalem on Palm Sunday.

X: I'm Agent X:

Y: I'm Agent Y.

X and Y: *(Together)* And we're the Shy Spies. Shhhhhhh.

X: We've come from our bosses...

Y: ...B and Q.

X and Y: *(Together)* And they've given us a mission to do.

X: We've been told to find out if Lazarus is in the crowd.

Y: And why do we want to find him?

X: Because he's a useful eye-witness. He'll be able to tell us what's going on.

Y: So what does he look like?

X: Well, I don't know, but he's got two sisters, and he'll probably be going wild!

Y: Oh yeah, my sisters make me wild.

X: No, Jesus miraculously raised him from the dead. He's probably the person here who's got the most to shout about!

Y: Pooey, won't he smell?

X: No, it happened about three months ago now. In fact Lazarus is part of the reason why there are so many people here today. Everybody's heard about Jesus raising him to life. It's why the authorities are hunting him down.

Y: Well, my sonic clue-finder will hunt him out!

He gets out the sonic clue-finder and tries to get it to work.

X: *(Fed up)* Well?

Y: Er, I think the elastic band has snapped.

X: Anyway there are some clues in the Code Book.

Get someone to read John 12.12–19. Use the Might come in handy section to get clued up beforehand.

Y: Can't see Lazarus at the moment. Maybe these people in the crowd can help us.

The Spies ask the crowd the following questions. When the questions have been answered, Shy Spies exit, commiserating that they didn't find Lazarus.

?

▷ Why are people waving palm branches and shouting Scriptures? (The Shy Spies can't understand what would make people do that.)
▷ It's five days before Passover. What's Passover all about?
▷ Who is Jesus? Where is he from? Why has everyone come to see him?
▷ There was a big procession the other day when Pilate arrived in Jerusalem. Who is he? Where is he from?

Try it!

A moving story: Palm Sunday procession

LEADER: Shame we didn't find Lazarus.

LAZARUS: *(Entering from the back of church)* Excuse me.

LEADER: He could have told us what it felt like to be part of that crowd.

LAZARUS: *(Coming forward)* Excuse me.

LEADER: Do you mind? I'm trying to do a link here.

LAZARUS: Yes, but you said you wanted to find Lazarus.

LEADER: So we did. But the Shy Spies couldn't find him, so we'll just have to get on with it. *(Turning back to congregation)*. Anyway, if we knew what it was like, then maybe we could recreate it in a small way...

LAZARUS: *(Interrupting)* But I'm Lazarus.

LEADER: You are?

LAZARUS: Yes.

LEADER: What, as in the 'dead once and now not dead' Lazarus?

LAZARUS: The very same!

LEADER: This is great! You can help us recreate what that experience was like.

LAZARUS: OK. But to do that we're going to need to get you cheering and singing and clapping.

Lazarus organises everybody into the crowd. To sing, you could use the tune of 'Oh When the Saints Go Marching In' and change the words to 'Oh When the Lord comes Riding In.' You will need instruments – get a tame trumpeter to play. Hand out shakers, drums, tambourines and anything that makes a loud noise.

Provide things to wave: palm leaves made from thin card, or real branches, or bits of fake Christmas tree work well. You could use scarves or dusters. Lazarus can give away some of his bandages!

Practice a Palestinian Wave (like a Mexican Wave but more holy.) This goes from the back to the front of the church. Practice a clapping rhythm, with a shout for Jesus at the end. Or you could chant: 'God bless the One who comes in the name of the Lord!'

LEADER: We need to start singing, because, ladies and gentlemen, boys and girls, the King is coming to visit our church this morning.

Sing the song. As it ends, lead the congregation in a chant. As the chant reaches the climax, someone playing Jesus should enter the church, maybe riding a bike or a scooter. As he moves down the middle of the church, through the crowd, get the Palestinian Wave going.

Meditation: stony silence

LEADER: Thanks Lazarus. That was great! Now imagine that – only thousands of times bigger. Imagine that in the city of Jerusalem.

As we heard earlier, even the stones wanted to shout with joy when Jesus came in. Let's be quiet now and think about that.

Give each person a stone to hold.

Look at me.

Normally you don't notice me.

You tread on me on your way to Jerusalem as you pick your way down the hilly path.

You don't look at the ground as you descend the Mount of Olives, instead you see the Golden Gate.

But I am here. Even though you barely see me.

I am here, and I know that you can feel me.

Feel me. I am unique.

There is no other stone like me.

To you, perhaps, every stone is the same.

But my colour, my smoothness, my rough edges are all my own.

I am here, but you want to ignore me.

All I do is make you uncomfortable.

And you think of me as dead, unfeeling.

But I see you.

I see your dusty feet, calloused and hardened by the sun and the sand.

I see the palms in your hands, I see your eyes bright with hope,

Until you lay a cloak over me.

And then all I can do is listen.

I hear the shouts, the chatter, the build-up of excitement for this new Deliverer-King.

I hear the carping and complaining of those who would dampen your spirits.

I feel the hardness of the donkey's hooves as our Rescuer approaches.

I hear his words of love for Jerusalem, and see his tears of pain.

And you think that I am silent.

But I, whose birth is lost in the beginning of time, I, who will outlast you all, I am shouting, too.

Live it!

LEADER: We've seen the crowd shout, we've heard the different accounts, we've talked to a very special member of the crowd that day, and we've even imagined the stones shouting out. I wonder what would happen if the stones in this church shouted out every Sunday? Just imagine what they would say if they could talk.

Gordon gets excited

GORDON: Some of us can.

LEADER: Gordon! Is that you?

GORDON: Of course it's me.

LEADER: We were just talking about stones. About how Jesus said the stones of Jerusalem would shout out.

GORDON: Quite a few of them did, you know. Well, that's what we gargoyles believe.

LEADER: Did they wave their palm leaves as well?

GORDON: Don't be daft. They're stones. They haven't got any hands.

LEADER: No, stupid of me.

GORDON: The most we can do is wobble our moss back and forth. Anyway, like I said, us gargoyles, we tell the stories of how the stones of the Temple gave a great shout that morning. Only no-one could hear it because everyone else was yelling so loud.

LEADER: A bit like us this morning. Did you hear us?

GORDON: Of course I heard you. You woke me up.

LEADER: You were asleep?

GORDON: Well, I had a late night. I was out clubbing with my gargoyle friends.

LEADER: Where do gargoyles go at night, then?

GORDON: We go out on the tiles, of course.

LEADER: I wish I hadn't asked.

GORDON: Anyway, you haven't half been making a lot of noise down there this morning.

LEADER: Well, we've been excited.

GORDON: How come you don't shout like that most Sundays?

LEADER: I don't know. Maybe we're too reserved. Stiff upper lip, and all that.

GORDON: Or maybe you're not thinking straight. You know, every Sunday Jesus comes into this place. Every time two or three of you get together in here, Jesus walks in through the front door, as it were. Imagine that. Every week he enters this place in triumph.

LEADER: I suppose you're right.

GORDON: And what does he get from you lot? Hardly a murmur. Sometimes you're so wrapped up in your own thoughts that you don't even notice he's around.

LEADER: It's difficult. It's not like it was then. He's not riding on a donkey through the streets.

GORDON: Maybe not, but he's still here. And isn't that something to get excited about? Now, if you'll excuse me, I've got to catch up on my beauty sleep.

LEADER: Yes, well, that's going to take quite a lot of sleep if you ask me.

GORDON: *(Snores)*

LEADER: Gordon? Gordon? Oh, he's gone.

TakeAway: a stone

Encourage people to use the stone they've been given. Or they can use a bandage banner or Palm Sunday cross. Provide pens.

LEADER: Gordon's right, isn't he? Do we still get excited every Sunday? Do we get excited about Jesus coming into our church and being with us?

As we finish our service, let's remember what it is that gets us excited about Jesus. Maybe you'd like to write that down to remind you. We've got some stones *(or bandages, or palm crosses)* here that you could write on if you wanted.

Closing prayer

Please save us Lord

and make us part of your kingdom.

Jesus, our King, you bring rescue and recovery

from the dark side of life.

Keep us in step with your triumphal procession,

that, as your fans and followers, we may

bring hope, freedom, health, love and peace

to all people and places on this earth.

Amen

Might come in handy

About Palm Sunday

The triumphant entry to Jerusalem probably took place on the Sunday before the crucifixion. Jesus entered from the east, coming over the Mount of Olives from Bethany, where he was staying. He would have entered Jerusalem through a gate on the eastern side.

Jesus' entrance contrasts with one which must have occurred around that time on the opposite side of the city – the entrance of Pilate and the Roman army to attend the city during Passover. Each procession represented a different kind of king and a different kind of kingdom.

About Jerusalem

Jerusalem at the time was home to some 35,000 people, all packed tightly into a city of little over 230 acres.[3] It was a splendid city with magnificent buildings. Chief of these, of course, was the Temple, which was begun in 20BC but not actually finished until 63AD. It stood on a massive platform (around 144,000 square metres) which stood, at its highest point, 45 metres above the floor of the Kidron valley. Today the platform is still visible, but the Temple was destroyed by the Romans. The only part of Herod's Temple remaining is the Western or 'wailing' wall.

The city was split into two halves – the wealthy, including the king and the high priest, lived in the upper city. The poor lived in the valley in the lower city, and this was where most of the commerce was conducted.

About Lazarus

Lazarus lived in Bethany with his sisters Martha and Mary. He was evidently a close friend of Jesus (Jn 11.3, 5, 11, 36) and Jesus raised him from the dead after he had been dead for four days (Jn. 11.17, 39; cf. vv 13–14). The raising of Lazarus caused many people to follow Jesus; but it also spurred Jesus' enemies into action (Jn. 11.45–53). The crowd which came to welcome Jesus into Jerusalem came largely because of the reports of Lazarus's resurrection. Indeed, there were plots to kill Lazarus as well (Jn. 12.9–11) – which is a bit unfair on someone who has only just come back from the dead.

Lazarus had a meal with Jesus and the others the night before Jesus entered Jerusalem. There his sister Mary anointed the feet of Jesus in preparation for Jesus' burial (Jn. 12.1–12:11). Jesus stayed with Lazarus and his sisters during his last week in Jerusalem. The event was significant for the early church, which called Bethany Lazarion, Greek for 'the place of Lazarus.'

---

3 That's less than one square kilometre for the non-farmers among you.

Getting ready

A week (or more) before

Questions

- [ ] Put questions on Power-point or notice sheet

PairTalk

- [ ] Put the list of descriptions of Jesus (e.g. the Messiah, etc.) and the two questions on Powerpoint or print out on noticesheet

Shy Spies

- [ ] Gather props and cos-tumes: coats, hats, shades, sonic clue-finder
- [ ] Allocate parts of X, Y, Laza-rus and Jesus (others if you want), distribute scripts

Palm Sunday procession

- [ ] Prepare music and musi-cians
- [ ] Print out alternative lyrics to *Oh when the saints go marching in*
- [ ] Gather percussion instru-ments
- [ ] Gather palm branches or things to wave, e.g. scarves, dusters, bandages
- [ ] Scooter or bike for Jesus

Meditation: stony silence

- [ ] Collect stones – one for each person

Gordon gets excited

- [ ] Copy script

TakeAway: a stone

- [ ] Stones or bandages or palm crosses and pens

An hour (or more) before

- [ ] Arrange seating and set – create clear wide aisle for path winding down Mount of Olives

Shy Spies

- [ ] Put props and costumes in place

Palm Sunday procession

- [ ] Put props and instruments in place

Meditation: stony silence

- [ ] Put stones in place

Gordon gets excited

- [ ] Set-up for Gordon (microphone, statue, etc. as required)

TakeAway: a stone

- [ ] Put resources in place

Celebrations!

Good Friday

3. GOOD FRIDAY

Title: Have I got news for you!
Aim: To think about why Jesus died and to feel the injustice of his death
Bible: John 18.28–19.16; 19.17–30

1. Want It!

The purpose here is to
▷ understand the 'story so far'
▷ remember what had happened that week to Jesus

We do this by asking people to
▷ listen and ask questions

The tools we use are
▷ Have you got news for us?
▷ Interactive sketch: Jerusalem News report

2. Watch It!

The purpose here is to
▷ see how Pilate made his mind up about Jesus
▷ see the injustice of Jesus' death

We do this by asking people to
▷ watch or take part in drama

The tools we use are
▷ A moving story: Pilate makes his mind up

3. Try It!

The purpose here is to
▷ understand why Jesus was sentenced to death
▷ feel the injustice of his death

We do this by asking people to
▷ talk and listen
▷ make a cross and tombstone
▷ hold a nightlight and pray

The tools we use are
▷ PairTalk: it's not fair
▷ Comment: no accident
▷ Make and listen: the cross
▷ Make and listen: the tomb
▷ Candlelit meditation

4. Live It!

4. Live it!
The purpose here is get people to
▷ realise that Jesus took their place and died for their sins
▷ tell others what they've learnt at this service

We do this by asking people to
▷ listen to the leader's comment

The tools we use are
▷ Comment: have I got news for you?
▷ Closing prayer: Jesus' prayer for us

Running order

When	What	Who
	Want it!	
	Have you got news for us?	
	Interactive sketch: Jerusalem TV News report	
	Watch it!	
	A moving story: Pilate makes his mind up	
	Try it!	
	PairTalk: it's not fair	
	Comment: no accident	
	Make and listen: the cross	
	Make and listen: the tomb	
	Candlelit meditation	
	Live it!	
	Comment: Have I got news for you!	
	Closing prayer	

Want it!

Have you got news for us?

LEADER: Good morning. This morning, have I got news for you? Oh yes, but first, have you got news for us?

> ▷ What's the news in your house?
> ▷ What's the news in our town?
> ▷ What's the news in the world? Has anyone listened to it? What's happening?

Interactive sketch: Jerusalem TV News report

LEADER: Imagine waking up in Jerusalem, just under two thousand years ago. On that morning, the city was abuzz with gossip. There were no newspapers in those days, so all the news was passed on by people talking to one another.

And the news in Jerusalem that morning was of the arrest of Jesus. But what if they had had news reporters? How would they would report it? To find out, let's turn to our reporter on the scene, Isaiah ben Kingsley.

Enter ISAIAH. He is a classic TV news reporter. He holds a microphone. He can either learn his script, or read it from a clipboard.

ISAIAH: Thank you. There's been sensational news in Jerusalem overnight. The rebel preacher and teacher, Jesus of Nazareth, was arrested last night while praying in the Garden of Gethsemane, an olive grove just to the east of Jerusalem.

It appears that Jesus had gone there with his followers to pray, following a meal in the city. He was identified by a former disciple, Judas Iscariot, and then arrested by the Temple guards. It is understood that he has already been tried by the Jewish authorities and has now been taken to the Roman Governor.

LEADER: How have the people taken the news, Isaiah?

ISAIAH: Well, let's ask a few of the people here this morning, shall we?

Interview members of the congregation as if they were contemporary eye-witnesses. The answers should not be scripted, although it's a good idea to warn some people beforehand!

> ▷ Are you a follower of this Jesus? Why?
> ▷ Were you waving palms in the crowd when he entered Jerusalem last Sunday?
> ▷ Did you see him clear the Temple?
> ▷ Is he someone special – or is he a threat? He claims to be the Son of God...

ISAIAH: Overall, there seems to have been a big change in public opinion. Just last week, you'll recall the people welcomed Jesus into the city like some kind of conquering hero. Now they seem less certain about him. It seems as if, now he's been arrested, they've given up on him.

LEADER: What about his followers?

ISAIAH: They've disappeared. We did think that some of them were in the courtyard last night, but they denied knowing Jesus. So it looks here as though the whole movement is collapsing.

LEADER: What will happen to him now?

ISAIAH: That's a good question. No-one knows for sure, because, as we all know, this city is governed by the Romans. So the High Priest can say what he wants, but unless the Roman Governor, Pontius Pilate, agrees to it, nothing is going to happen.

LEADER: So where is Jesus now?

ISAIAH: He's being taken to the Roman Governor, who is in the Palace at the west side of Jerusalem. For now, all we can do is wait and see. Isaiah Ben Kingsley, Jerusalem, for the Early Morning News. *(Exits.)*

LEADER: *(to congregation)* So, we can see that if we'd woken in Jerusalem on that morning, there would have been lots for us to talk about. The people would have been wondering who this Jesus was, and what was going to happen next.

Watch it!

A moving story: Pilate makes his mind up

This is a dramatised rendering of the dialogue recorded in John 18.28–19.1. It's taken from the Contemporary English Version.

The trial of Jesus before Pilate takes place in two main locations – Inside Pilate's Palace and Outside Pilate's Palace. For this you will need to use two locations at opposite ends of the church.

Choose a place up front for the 'Inside' of Pilate's Palace. Put a big chair here and have it furnished as best you can, use screens, throws, etc.

The second location is 'Outside' the palace: the palace courtyard. Make a space at the opposite end of the church. You want the audience to get the sense of movement between the two.

Of course, the simplest way of doing this is to have two readers read the relevant passages from each location. But it's better to re-enact the scene. This does not need a lot of preparation, but you will need some copies of the script.

You will need people for the following roles:
▷ *Pilate*

▷ *Two Roman guards*

▷ *Jewish leaders*

▷ *Crowd*

▷ *Jesus*

It's best to choose someone to play the main parts (NARRATOR, PILATE and JESUS) in advance. Then you can give them their script and they can read it through. They do not have to learn the lines. (Although it would be great if they did!)

The Roman guards, Jewish leaders and the crowd can be allocated and guided on the day. You will need to shepherd some of the people through their parts. If you want to be free to narrate it, get someone to be your Stage Director and let them show these groups what to do at the right time.

Get some adults to be the Jewish leaders. Get the children to be the crowd.

NARRATOR: It was early in the morning when Jesus was taken to the building where the Roman governor stayed.

Jesus is brought by the Jewish leaders and crowd to the Outside area – probably best to bring him in through the front door first.

NARRATOR: But the crowd *(this includes the Jewish leaders)* waited outside. Any of them who had gone inside would have become unclean and would not be allowed to eat the Passover meal. Pilate came out.

Pilate goes from the Inside area to the Outside area.

PILATE: What charges are you bringing against this man?

JEWISH LEADERS: He is a criminal! That's why we brought him to you.

PILATE: Take him and judge him by your own laws.

JEWISH LEADERS: We are not allowed to put anyone to death.

NARRATOR: And so what Jesus said about his death would soon come true. Pilate then went back inside. He called Jesus over.

Pilate sends two Roman guards to fetch Jesus and bring him Inside. Jesus stands in front of Pilate.

PILATE: Are you the king of the Jews?

JESUS: Are you asking this on your own or did someone tell you about me?

PILATE: You know I'm not a Jew! Your own people and the chief priests brought you to me. What have you done?

JESUS: My kingdom doesn't belong to this world. If it did, my followers would have fought to keep me from being handed over to the Jewish leaders.

PILATE: So you are a king.

JESUS: You are saying that I am a king. I was born into this world to tell about the truth. And everyone who belongs to the truth knows my voice.

PILATE: What is truth?

NARRATOR: Pilate went back out.

Pilate goes Outside to talk to the Jewish leaders and crowd.

PILATE: I don't find this man guilty of anything! And since I usually set a prisoner free for you at Passover, would you like for me to set free the king of the Jews?

JEWISH LEADERS: No, not him! We want Barabbas.

Pilate goes Inside and watches the Roman guards put a crown of thorns on Jesus and a robe.

NARRATOR: Now Barabbas was a terrorist. Pilate gave orders for Jesus to be beaten with a whip. The soldiers made a crown out of thorn branches and put it on Jesus. Then they put a purple robe on him. They came up to him and said, 'Hey, you king of the Jews!' They also hit him with their fists.

Once again Pilate went out.

Pilate goes Outside

PILATE: I will have Jesus brought out to you again. Then you can see for yourselves that I have not found him guilty.

Pilate claps his hands and the guards bring Jesus Outside.

NARRATOR: Jesus came out, wearing the crown of thorns and the purple robe.

PILATE: Here is the man!

NARRATOR: When the chief priests and the Temple police saw him, they started yelling:

JEWISH LEADERS: Nail him to a cross! Nail him to a cross!

PILATE: You take him and nail him to a cross! I don't find him guilty of anything.

JEWISH LEADERS: He claimed to be the Son of God! Our Jewish Law says that he must be put to death.

NARRATOR: When Pilate heard this, he was terrified.

Pilate, accompanied by the guards and Jesus, goes back Inside.

PILATE: Where are you from?

Jesus does not answer.

PILATE: Why won't you answer my question? Don't you know that I have the power to let you go free or to nail you to a cross?

JESUS: If God had not given you the power, you couldn't do anything at all to me. But the one who handed me over to you did something even worse.

Pilate goes Outside again.

PILATE: I want to set this man free.

JEWISH LEADERS: If you set this man free, you are no friend of the Emperor! Anyone who claims to be a king is an enemy of the Emperor.

NARRATOR: When Pilate heard this, he brought Jesus out.

Pilate claps his hands again. Jesus is brought back Outside.

NARRATOR: He sat down on the judge's bench at the place known as 'the Stone Pavement.' In Aramaic this pavement is called 'Gabbatha.' It was about noon on the day before Passover, and Pilate said to the crowd:

PILATE: Look at your king!

JEWISH LEADERS: Kill him! Kill him! Nail him to a cross!

PILATE: So you want me to nail your king to a cross?

JEWISH LEADERS: The Emperor is our king!

NARRATOR: Then Pilate handed Jesus over to be nailed to a cross.

Pilate goes back inside. The Jewish leaders, the guards and Jesus exit in the opposite direction.

Try it!

LEADER: So we've seen Jesus' trial. I wonder what you thought of that. Pilate said he'd done nothing wrong and still he was condemned to death.

PairTalk: it's not fair

Ask the people to work in pairs. Put the following questions in a notice sheet or on Powerpoint. You can choose whether to take feedback from discussions or whether to move on with the story. If you decide to take feedback, try to divide the time between getting people to understand intellectually what happened, and emotionally, how it would have felt.

▷ What did Pilate think of Jesus?
▷ Why did Pilate sentence him to death?
▷ How would have felt if this had happened to you?
▷ Are there any times in your life when you have been unfairly judged or treated?
▷ Have you ever taken the punishment that was due to someone else? Why did it happen? How did you feel?

Comment: no accident

LEADER: It's important to remember that none of this was an accident. Jesus' whole purpose in life (and death) was to save people from their sins. Many people had recognised this before the event and Jesus himself did, too. Even before Jesus was born, thirty-three years earlier, an angel had told Joseph:

ANGEL: Joseph, the baby that Mary will have is from the Holy Spirit. Go ahead and marry her. Then after her baby is born, name him Jesus, because he will save his people from their sins (Mt. 1.20–21).

LEADER: The name Jesus means 'the Lord saves.' Just three years before, John the Baptist had said to everyone:

JOHN: Here is the Lamb of God, who takes away the sin of the world (Jn. 1.29)!

LEADER: And just last night Jesus would have been saying to his friends, when he offered them the wine:

JESUS: Take this and drink it. This is my blood, and with it God makes his agreement with you. It will be poured out, so that many people will have their sins forgiven (Mt. 26.26–28).

Make and listen: the cross

LEADER: Now we're going to take the story further – and this is where it gets sad. Because Pilate sentenced Jesus to death. We're going to hear that part of the story now. But while you're listening to the reading, I want you to do something.

Jesus was killed on a cross. And that's why the symbol of the cross is so important to Christians. Because it reminds us of his death.

DIY

▷ Introduce Bible reading John 19.17–30

▷ Get people to make a cross out of tinfoil as they listen

You will find some tin foil in front of you. What I want you to do now is to take this foil and make a little cross with it.

I want us to do that quietly.

Let's make our foil into the shape of a cross.

Bible: John 19.17–30

Everyone makes the foil into a cross whilst listening to the reading.

Make and listen: the tomb

LEADER: After he died, Jesus was taken down from the cross, and buried in a tomb. In those days, tombs were above the ground, often hollowed out from caves. They put Jesus in one of these and rolled a huge stone across the entrance.

DIY

▷ Introduce Bible reading John 19.38–42

▷ Get people to turn their tinfoil crosses into little 'tombstones'

Let's think about that now, and as we do, let's change the shape of the foil in our hands.

I want you to roll it into a ball, to represent the stone across the entrance of the tomb.

Bible: John 19.38–42

Everyone makes the foil into a stone whilst listening to the reading. At the end of the reading, ask people to put silver foil 'tombstones' in a certain place. If you have an Easter garden display, they could pile them up by the entrance to the tomb. This could be done to a background of music.

As they put down the foil tombstones, they pick up a ready-lit nightlight. Invite people to stand around the church with their nightlight. Make sure the room is as dark as it can be at this point.

You could sing a very simple song – one that needs no words so people don't have to hold hymnbooks or sheets in front of them. Alternatively, your choir or music group could sing as people stand.

Candlelit meditation

Heavenly Father,

As we remember the death of your son, Jesus Christ, on the cross,

help us to understand how it must have felt.

People wanted to get rid of Jesus,

Even though he had done nothing wrong.

It wasn't fair that he should die –

But still he took the punishment.

He took the blame.

Help us to understand why it happened:

That it was for all of us that Jesus died,

So that many people would have their sins forgiven.

This is difficult for us to grasp.

It happened many years ago.

Make it real for us today.

Amen

Live it!

LEADER: We are remembering a sad day; a day with a lot of questions – why did it happen? What does it mean? And why is it a Good Friday?

We've seen how Jesus was unfairly judged, executed and put into a tomb. That's horrible – that's not 'good' at all. So why isn't this Bad Friday?

No-one really knows where the phrase 'Good Friday' comes from. It's been called many things. Some countries call it Great or Holy Friday. The Anglo-Saxons called it Long Friday. What we do know is that Friday was viewed as a special day from the very earliest days of Christianity.

They knew what happened on that Friday was really special. Even though what happened was horrible for Jesus, it was good news for the rest of us.

Because he's rescued us. Imagine if you were going to die, if you were sentenced to death like Jesus, and then someone came in and they'd taken your place. You'd think that was good news.

And that's the best way of remembering today. What happened to Jesus was very bad . But because he died, we can all live forever. And that makes it a good Friday, I suppose.

DIY

▷ Why 'Good' Friday?

▷ Significant day for the early church.

▷ What happened to Jesus was good news for us

▷ Because he died, we can all live

Have I got news for you?

LEADER: Well, that's the news today, this Friday. It's Good News, I'm glad to say. Although, it may not sound like it to begin with.

We've found out that around two thousand years ago, Jesus was unfairly sentenced to death. Worse than that, we are implicated in his death.

His death didn't just happen because he angered the Jewish leaders. It didn't just happen because Pilate had to make a decision in the most chaotic of circumstances. People killed God the Son, because he got in their way.

We too, if we are honest, think God gets in the way – of us leading life the way we want to. That's sin, in a nutshell.

Jesus wanted to save us from that. He knew that if we want to really live, we can't do it without God. And he wants us to really live – forever. Like God intended.

He bore the brunt of people's anger towards God, and God's anger at our sin. He got caught in the middle, and willingly took it on the chin. He stood in our place and – have I got news for you? – he did it so that we could get off scot free!

That's why it's Good Friday!

But it gets better still, because we know that isn't the end of the story. God raised him from death back to life – and that's something we'll celebrate on Sunday.

For now we want you to take the good news away with you.

Jesus prayed for us the night before he died. Let's stay quiet for a moment as we think about all we've learnt. Then, we will hear the prayer that Jesus prayed for us. And then we'll blow out our lights, and leave, in silence.

Closing prayers: Jesus' prayer for us

I am praying for everyone who will have faith because of what my followers will say about me. I want all of them to be one with each other, just as I am one with you, Father and you are one with me. I also want them to be one with us. Then the people of this world will believe that you sent me (Jn.17.20–21).

People leave in silence.

Might come in handy

About Good Friday

From the earliest times, Friday was a special day for Christians, who kept every Friday as a feast day. The Friday before Easter – the Friday which marked the anniversary of Christ's death – came to be called the 'Great' or the 'Holy' Friday. The origin of the term Good Friday is not certain, it may have come from the German name 'God's Friday' (Gottes Freitag).

Jesus' trial: the ins and outs

The diagram below shows the movements of Jesus, Pilate and the Jewish leaders during Jesus' trial.

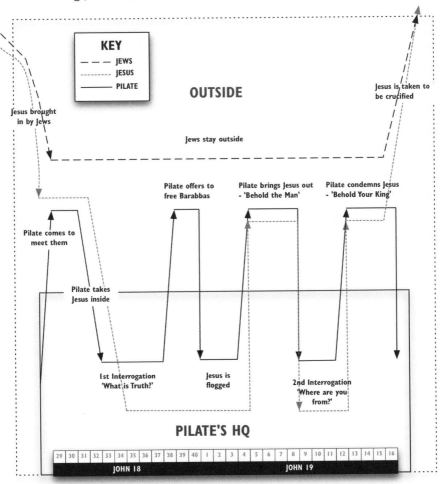

KEY
– – – JEWS
·········· JESUS
——— PILATE

OUTSIDE

Jesus is taken to be crucified

Jesus brought in by Jews

Jews stay outside

Pilate offers to free Barabbas

Pilate brings Jesus out - 'Behold the Man'

Pilate condemns Jesus - 'Behold Your King'

Pilate comes to meet them

Pilate takes Jesus inside

1st Interrogation 'What is Truth?'

Jesus is flogged

2nd Interrogation 'Where are you from?'

PILATE'S HQ

| 29 | 30 | 31 | 32 | 33 | 34 | 35 | 36 | 37 | 38 | 39 | 40 | 1 | 2 | 3 | 4 | 5 | 6 | 7 | 8 | 9 | 10 | 11 | 12 | 13 | 14 | 15 | 16 |

JOHN 18   JOHN 19

Getting Ready

A week (or more) before

Questions

- ☐ Put questions on Power-point or notice sheet

Jerusalem TV News report

- ☐ Allocate part of reporter
- ☐ Copy script for Isaiah ben Kingsley
- ☐ Find clipboard

A moving story: Pilate makes his mind up

- ☐ Allocate some or all of parts
- ☐ Make copies of scripts
- ☐ Gather any props/costumes

Group discussion

- ☐ Put questions onto Power-point or in noticesheet

Make and listen

- ☐ Get silver foil
- ☐ Get nightlights

An hour (or more) before

A moving story: Pilate makes his mind up

- ☐ Arrange seating and set – create two focal points at each end of the church for Inside Pilate's Palace and Outside Pilate's Palace

Make and listen

- ☐ Put silver foil in place

Candlelit meditation

- ☐ Put nightlights and matches in place

Easter Sunday

4. EASTER DAY

Title: He's alive!
Aim: To convey the excitement of finding Jesus alive; to reinforce the fact of the resurrection
Bible: John 20.1–18

1. Want It!

The purpose here is to
- ▷ join in with the oldest celebration of the Christian Church
- ▷ take in the fact that Jesus rose from the dead

We do this by asking people to
- ▷ unravel the foil 'tombstones'
- ▷ repeat a refrain

The tools we use are
- ▷ Introduction: roll away the stone
- ▷ Easter declaration

2. Watch It!

The purpose here is to
- ▷ picture the events of Sunday morning
- ▷ understand what happened

We do this by asking people to
- ▷ watch a drama
- ▷ put a story together using clues

The tools we use are
- ▷ Drama: the other gardener
- ▷ The Shy Spies investigate: the mystery of the missing body

3. Try It!

The purpose here is to
- ▷ share the joy of the women and men on Easter morning
- ▷ understand that Jesus' resurrection means he has defeated death

We do this by asking people to
- ▷ discuss the reaction of the women and men
- ▷ reflect and pray

The tools we use are
- ▷ Discussion: the women and the men
- ▷ Reflection: why are you crying?
- ▷ Prayer: so many questions

4. Live It!

The purpose here is to
- ▷ recognise that Christ died in our place
- ▷ see how the early church responded to the resurrection
- ▷ recognise that resurrection is key to the life of the Church

We do this by asking people to
- ▷ listen and pray

The tools we use are
- ▷ Bible: the Easter fact file
- ▷ TakeAway: Easter wings
- ▷ Closing prayer

Running order

When	What	Who
	Want it!	
	Introduction: roll away the stone	
	Easter declaration	
	Watch it!	
	Drama: the other gardener	
	The Shy Spies investigate: the mystery of the missing body	
	Try it!	
	Discussion: the women and the men	
	Reflection: why are you crying?	
	Prayer: so many questions	
	Live it!	
	Bible: Easter fact file	
	TakeAway: Easter wings	
	Closing prayer: Easter in us	

Want it!

Introduction: roll away the stone

LEADER: Welcome to resurrection day!

Welcome to the greatest – and oldest – feast of the Christian Church.

Welcome to the day when death was defeated.

Welcome to the day when Jesus proved he was who he claimed to be.

Welcome to the day that changed the world forever!

Welcome to resurrection day!

He rose from the dead. This is what we celebrate today. A week ago we saw how he entered the city in triumph. Two days ago we saw how he died for us all.

The following section uses the silver foil stones made during the Good Friday service (p.44). If you did not do this, skip to the Easter declaration

---

LEADER: On Friday, we made crosses out of silver foil while listening to what happened to Jesus. Then we rolled the foil into balls to remind us of his burial in a cave, sealed with a tombstone.

Today, let's roll these tombstones away. Come and take them, then unroll the ball and look inside.

Congregation takes the silver stone and unwraps it. Inside each stone is a slip of paper saying: Jesus Christ is risen from the dead.

Easter declaration

LEADER: So together we say today:

ALL: Jesus Christ is risen from the dead!

LEADER: On the morning of that first Easter Day:

ALL: Jesus Christ is risen from the dead!

LEADER: The first Christians told what they had seen:

ALL: Jesus Christ is risen from the dead!

LEADER: Throughout the centuries the Church has proclaimed:

ALL: Jesus Christ is risen from the dead!

LEADER: Today in *[name of town]* we proclaim:

ALL: Jesus Christ is risen from the dead!

Watch it!

Drama: the other gardener

MANAGER: Ah Amos, come in. Would you like to take a seat?

AMOS: Thanks very much but I got quite a lot at home.

MANAGER: Right. Anyway, I wanted to see you about the garden.

AMOS: Ah. Yes, I'm very pleased with it. I think it's coming together nicely.

MANAGER: Amos, it's full of weeds.

AMOS: Weeds?

MANAGER: We in the Parks and Gardens department employ you to keep the garden spotless. To make it a thing of beauty.

AMOS: Arr. I done that all right.

MANAGER: Yes. Well, it depends on your concept of beauty really, doesn't it? I mean most people, for example, would agree that nettles are ugly. Whereas you, Amos, choose to feature them in special flower beds. Why have you deliberately filled three flower beds full of nettles?

AMOS: That's my sensory garden.

MANAGER: In what way is it sensory?

AMOS: You try touching it, you'll soon find out.

MANAGER: Nettles aren't flowers, Amos. They're weeds. As are dandelions. So why you've replaced the formal rose garden with dandelions is beyond me! They're weeds!

AMOS: Weeds! Weeds! You'll be telling me to get rid of the poison ivy next.

MANAGER: *(alarmed)* Poison ivy?

AMOS: Yes. I've trained it to grow all over the pergola. Looks lovely it does.

MANAGER: Why are you doing this?

AMOS: I'm working with nature, aren't I? I mean, you take your nettle. You knock him down, you bury him in the ground, he pops right up again. You just think you've got him down and then up he jumps. It's his nature. So I just thought, don't fight it, go with it. Turn him into a display.

MANAGER: But I don't want a display of nettles. I don't want a formal dandelion garden, or a poison-ivy covered pergola. I want my rose garden back!

AMOS: I was just trying to make it an interesting, challenging place to visit.

MANAGER: It's a graveyard! A garden of rest. People come here to visit the tombs of their loved ones, not get stung to death themselves. I mean, I walked through there this morning and the place was a mess! There were muddy footprints all over the place.

AMOS: Arr, well that's nothing to do with me. That'd be the guards.

MANAGER: Guards?

AMOS: The Roman guards by the tomb. I dunno what happened, but it looks like first they fell over, and then they got up and ran away. *(Thinks for a moment)* They must have been scared, 'cause they ran right through the nettle display. *(Assertively)* And I didn't move that stone either.

MANAGER: Stone? What stone?

AMOS: The big tombstone. You know the preacher fella who was laid in there couple of days ago? Someone's moved his stone and it weren't me. I couldn't roll a great big thing like that. Not with my back.

MANAGER: But this is serious! You mean to say someone's opened the grave?

AMOS: Well, it looks like some kind of 'splosion to me. Stone's been rolled away and something's blown all the heads off my prize thistles.

MANAGER: It must have been his followers!

AMOS: No. Weren't them. They were as shocked as anyone else. They arrived so fast they near knocked me into the ornamental clover patch. They told me he'd come back. Come back to life.

MANAGER: Nonsense!

AMOS: *(suspiciously)* You ask me, that tomb was opened from the inside.

MANAGER: *(sharply)* I didn't ask you. I wouldn't ask you anything. Not unless I wanted to know some useless weed-related information.

AMOS: *(hurt)* If that's how you feel, maybe you better ask that new gardener.

MANAGER: What new gardener?

AMOS: Don't you deny it. I saw him in the distance. I know we've had our creative differences, but there's no need to go appointing someone behind my back.

MANAGER: I haven't appointed any new gardeners.

AMOS: Oh. That's a bit odd.

MANAGER: It's a disaster! There were guards all over the place. They were supposed to keep him in there. To make sure this didn't happen.

AMOS: 'Keep him in', eh? So it is true.

MANAGER: I didn't say that.

AMOS: No, but you'm thinking it. Just like he said. Maybe you got your 'rose garden' after all.

MANAGER: This is serious. I'm going to have to speak to the authorities. We could lose our licence. I want the mess cleared up, and the garden put back just as if nothing has happened. Nothing has happened, right? *(He rushes out.)*

AMOS: *(thinking for a moment)* You knock him down, you bury him in the ground, he pops right up again. It's in his nature.

Exit.

The Shy Spies investigate: the mystery of the missing body

The idea here is to retell the Easter story using objects found around the church. The following clues should be hidden around the church:

 ▷ *Some spices*

 ▷ *A stone*

 ▷ *A torch*

 ▷ *A dictaphone or answerphone*

 ▷ *Some linen or sheets*

 ▷ *A padlock*

Enter the Shy Spies.

X: I'm Agent X:

Y: I'm Agent Y.

X and Y: *(Together)* And we're the Shy Spies. Shhhhhhh.

X: We've come from our bosses...

Y: ...B and Q.

X and Y: *(Together)* And they've given us a mission to do.

X: We're investigating a mystery. The mystery of the missing body.

Y: There was a body in the tomb. And now it's gone.

X: So what's happened?

Y: We've been told there are clues hidden around this church.

X: But how do we find them?

Y: Simple! I use my famous sonic clue-finder!

X: I don't know why you bother. You know it never works.

Y: Of course it does. I press this and pull this bit here and... *(nothing happens.)* Oh. It's run out of petrol.

X: We don't need that. We just need our secret spy helpers to find the clues.

Y: And remember – not a sound...

The Shy Spies send children and adults off around the church to find the clues. Each clue object has a sticker on it, or a label attached giving the Bible reference. When all the clues are assembled, the spies should get people to look up the verses in order and read them out. As the verses are read the Spies should piece together the story. The clues are as follows:

Clue	Significance	Bible reading
Spices	The women went to anoint the body.	Luke 24.1
Stone	The stone rolled away from the tomb entrance.	Luke 24.2–3
Torch	The angels' clothes glowed with light.	Luke 24.4–5
Answerphone	The women remembered Jesus' words	Luke 24.6–8
Linen	The women went to tell the apostles.	Luke 24.9–12
Padlock	Jesus appeared to them in a locked room	John 20.19–20

X: So this is the story.

Y: *(holding up spices)* Some women take spices to a tomb.

X: *(holding up stone)* The tomb is empty and the stone rolled away.

Y: *(holding up torch)* Two angels are there who tell them...

X: That the dead man has risen.

Y: *(holding up answerphone)* And they remembered what he said.

X: *(holding up linen)* So they ran back to the apostles and showed them the graveclothes.

Y: *(holding up padlock)* And later, Jesus appeared to them in a locked room.

X: That's the story as it really is.

Y: Now, you've got to work out, what does it mean?

X: We've got to go and report back to B & Q.

They exit.

Try it!

Discussion: the women and the men

Divide the congregation into groups of men and women. Then invite each group to discuss the following questions:

?

Women
▷ Which women were around when Jesus died (Jn. 19.25)?
▷ Why did some women go to the garden tomb (Lk. 24.1)?
▷ How was Mary feeling that morning (Jn. 20.11)?
▷ What do you think she felt like when she met the risen Jesus?
▷ If you were Mary, what sort of questions would you have wanted to ask him?

? **Men**
▷ Which men were around when Jesus died (Jn. 19.26–27, 19.38–42; Lk. 24.49)?
▷ Who came and found the empty tomb (Jn. 20.3–10)?
▷ How did the disciples react when the women told them Jesus had risen (Lk. 24.11)?
▷ How do you think they felt when they met him that evening (Jn. 20.19–23) ?
▷ What questions would you have wanted to ask the risen Jesus?

LEADER: The women thought they'd lost everything. On Friday the women saw Jesus die; on Sunday morning they didn't even have the body any more. But when they heard he was back, they must have felt overjoyed.

The men were in a locked room, hiding. They were afraid of what would happen to them. But now they ran straight to the tomb to look for themselves. They were no longer afraid.

It was obviously a moment of huge joy to both men and women, because Jesus rose from the dead, but it meant more than just that. The Shy Spies went away saying we've got to work out what Jesus' resurrection meant. What do you think it means?

We need no longer be afraid of death, because he's defeated it.

DIY
▷ The women had lost everything.
▷ The men were scared
▷ But Jesus' resurrection leaves us full of joy and no longer afraid of death.

Reflection: why are you crying?

Jesus asked, 'Why are you crying?'

Mary was crying because Jesus had died.

Do we cry for Jesus?

Jesus asked, 'Who are you looking for?'

Mary was looking for Jesus.

Do we look for Jesus?

Jesus said, 'Mary.'

Mary answered, 'Teacher.'

Mary recognised Jesus.

Do we recognise Jesus?

Jesus said, 'Go and tell my brothers.'

Mary told others about Jesus.

Do we tell others about Jesus?

Prayer: so many questions

Lord Jesus, it's difficult to imagine you really being dead, and then coming alive again.

(Pause)

We've tried to imagine what it would be like for Mary and the women.

Mary thought you were dead, but there you were, alive and talking to her.

If it were to happen to us, we'd have so many questions:

What is it like to die?

Have you seen heaven and hell?

Are you really alive?

Can you stay forever?

(Pause)

We've tried to imagine what it would be like for Peter and John and the disciples.

They ran away from you when you needed them most. They felt bad.

They didn't trust the women. They had to see for themselves.

If it were to happen to us, we'd have so many apologies to make.

Lord, forgive us.

We didn't stick up for you.

We ran away.

We're so sorry.

(Pause)

You didn't mention any of that. You didn't blame. You didn't accuse. You said:

Don't you know it had to happen? There had to be suffering before glory.

I'm going back to our Father, but I'm sending you out.

Receive the Holy Spirit; forgive people their sins.

You said: Do you have something to eat?

We love you Lord, and are so glad that your death wasn't the end.

Stay with us, and by your Holy Spirit, now as then, breathe on us and warm our hearts with your presence.

Amen

Live It

Bible: Easter fact file

LEADER: This is what the first Christians believed about the resurrection: it was fact not fiction. It happened. It was real. Something transformed the ragged bunch hiding in the upper room into a world-changing force.

Let's hear what some of those first Christians had to say on the subject.

These should be read out by different voices.

Peter said: *(a reader reads Acts 2.22–24, 31-32)*

Peter and John said: *(a reader reads Acts 4.9–12)*

The apostles said: *(several readers read Acts 5.29–31)*

Paul said: *(a reader reads 1 Corinthians 15.3–8)*

LEADER: Many people saw him. Many people knew what had happened. It was a fact which the early church went back to time and time again in their preaching and teaching: Jesus rose from the dead.

They even changed their Sabbath to be on the first day of the week – Sunday – because it was the day of Christ's coming back to life.

Why did they go on about it? Because they knew that it proved Jesus was who he said he was. They knew that he had defeated death. It is the resurrection that gives us hope of a new, eternal life: as Christ rose, so will we.

As Paul said 'If you confess with your mouth, "Jesus is Lord," and believe in your heart that God raised him from the dead, you will be saved' (Rom. 10.9).

TakeAway: Easter wings

If you have already used tin foil in the Good Friday service, use the same piece. Otherwise give out new pieces of tin foil.

LEADER: As you reflect on Jesus' resurrection this morning, I want you to take the silver foil one last time. Smooth it out and then scrunch it up in the middle to look like wings. George Herbert, a vicar and a poet, wrote a shape poem hundreds of years ago, called Easter-wings: two verses written in the shape of wings. In the poem he asked God to raise him up and give him 'Easter-wings.'

If you want you can read Herbert's poem here.

LEADER: Let's ask the Lord to raise us to life today.

Lord you made us rich, but somehow in our foolishness, we threw it all away.

Time and again, men and women have chosen to desert you,

Preferring poverty to being a child of God the King.

With you, let us rise like a lark to sing that

In the battle between death and the King of Life: You win!

And we have the enormous privilege of travelling in the wake of your victory.

As rebels we pitted ourselves against you.

Lord, we could have been fat with your love,

but somehow in our foolishness, we turned our heads away and became thin.

Time and again, men and women have chosen to starve themselves,

Preferring hunger to being a child of God the King.

With you, let us rise, hanging on to your coat-tails as you escape the cold clutches of the cave, neatly dodging tragedy and death.

Let us fly with you with Easter wings.

Easter in us. Raise us to life today.

Closing prayer: Easter in us

Jesus, our Lord, we praise you that nothing could keep you dead in the grave.

You are stronger than death and the devil.

Help us to remember that there is nothing to be afraid of,

Because you are alive and by our side.

Amen

Might come in handy

About Easter

Easter is the oldest and greatest feast of the Christian Church.

In the ancient church it was the traditional day of baptism – candidates would stay awake on a vigil on the Saturday night, then be baptized early on Easter day and receive communion. This tradition dates back at least to the early 200s AD and probably reaches a lot further.

The night before Easter was celebrated by illuminating the church all night – in some places the entire city or town kept the lamps or candles burning all night as well.

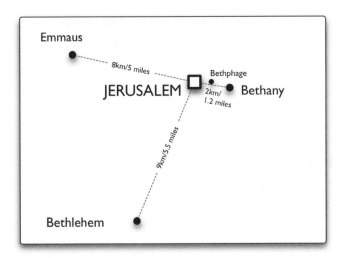

About Mary

We don't know much about her past, but we do know Jesus cast seven demons out of her. She was at the cross when he was crucified (Mk. 15.40) and then went with other women to the tomb to anoint him. Mary Magdalene was the first to see the risen Christ (Jn. 20.11ff.) Tradition says that she later went to Ephesus where she died.

Easter wings

This is the title of one of George Herbert's pattern poems. Pattern poems are shaped to resemble an object. You can find a copy at: http://www.ccel.org/h/herbert/temple/Easterwings.html

Getting ready

A week (or more) before

Questions

- [ ] Put questions on Power-point or notice sheet

Roll away the stone

- [ ] If you made silver foil tomb-stones on Good Friday, unravel each one and put a slip of paper inside saying 'Jesus Christ is risen from the dead'

Drama: The other gardener

- [ ] Allocate parts, copy scripts, rehearse
- [ ] Gather any props or cos-tumes

The Shy Spies Easter treasure hunt

- [ ] Gather props and cos-tumes: coats, hats, shades, sonic clue-finder
- [ ] Allocate parts of X, Y, dis-tribute scripts
- [ ] Print clues
- [ ] Find way to display clues

Discussion: the women and the men

- [ ] Prepare discussion ques-tions on Powerpoint or print on noticesheet

TakeAway: Easter wings

- [ ] Look at poem

An hour (or more) before

- [ ] Arrange seating and set

Introduction: roll away the stone

- [ ] Put silver foil tombstones in place

Drama: the other gardener

- [ ] Put props and costume in place

The Shy Spies investigate: the mystery of the missing body

- [ ] Put props, costumes and clues in place
- [ ] Hide Easter treasure/clues

Celebrations!

Pentecost

5. PENTECOST

Title: Wish you were here!
Aim: To welcome God's Spirit
Bible: Acts 2.1–13

1. Want It!

The purpose here is to
- ▷ share a sense of international festivity
- ▷ think about the amazing things God does

We do this by asking people to
- ▷ speak a different language
- ▷ talk about miracles

The tools we use are
- ▷ Game: where in the world?
- ▷ PairTalk: seen any miracles lately?

2. Watch It!

The purpose here is to
- ▷ picture the event of Pentecost
- ▷ look at the event from different perspectives

We do this by asking people to
- ▷ watch and take part in the drama
- ▷ answer questions

The tools we use are
- ▷ A moving story: Pentecost
- ▷ The Shy Spies investigate: strange times in Jerusalem

3. Try It!

The purpose here is to
- ▷ think how about much they welcome God's Spirit
- ▷ confess to keeping God at a distance

We do this by asking people to
- ▷ think and pray
- ▷ re-enact the response to Peter's sermon

The tools we use are
- ▷ Meditation: inside out
- ▷ A moving response: Peter's sermon
- ▷ International song
- ▷ Prayers for the nations

4. Live It!

The purpose here is to
- ▷ retell the Pentecost story
- ▷ give people the confidence to tell others about church
- ▷ celebrate the Church's birthday

We do this by asking people to
- ▷ write/draw a postcard
- ▷ listen to Gordon
- ▷ sing/give a present/eat cake!

The tools we use are
- ▷ TakeAway: Pentecost postcard
- ▷ Gordon speaks pigeon
- ▷ Birthday celebrations
- ▷ Blessing

Running order

When	What	Who
	Want it!	
	Game: where in the world...?	
	PairTalk: seen any miracles lately?	
	Watch it!	
	A moving story: Pentecost	
	The Shy Spies investigate: strange times in Jerusalem	
	Try it!	
	Meditation: inside out	
	A moving response: Peter's sermon	
	International song	
	Prayers for the nations	
	Live it!	
	TakeAway: Pentecost postcard	
	Gordon speaks pigeon	
	Birthday celebrations	
	Blessing	

Want it!

Game: Where In the world...?

Arrange the seats in a circle. Decorate the church with flags and anything that will give it an international feel. As people enter the church, give them a label with 'Hello' written on it in one of five different languages. The languages are Arabic, Turkish, Italian, Greek and Hebrew.

   ▷ *Arabic: Al Salaam A'alaykum*

   ▷ *Turkish: Merhaba*

   ▷ *Italian: Ciao!*

   ▷ *Greek: Kalimera*

   ▷ *Hebrew: Shalom*

Invite people to walk round and look at people's labels. Their task is to find out which language the word comes from, and then to use it to greet people.

DIY

▷Introduction and welcome

▷Find out if there are people in congregation from another country

▷Ask them how to say 'God has done wonderful things!' in their language

▷Ask 'Has anyone ever witnessed a miracle?'

LEADER: Welcome to our church today, as we celebrate Pentecost, the day the Church was born! The languages on your labels are the languages of the 'Pentecost' countries. They're the modern-day versions of the countries or the Roman Empire and beyond.

You can show this using the map on p.76.

   ▷ There are 202 million people who speak Arabic.
   ▷ There are 56 million people who speak Turkish.
   ▷ There are 63 million who speak Italian.
   ▷ There are 12 million people who speak Greek.
   ▷ There are 5 million people who speak Hebrew.

?   ▷ How many languages can you speak?

Invite people to come and give greetings in their own language. Ask them how they would they say, 'God has done wonderful things!'

LEADER: If you can speak another language, French, for example, would you be able to talk to a French person about the wonderful things God has done? Or would it take a miracle to enable you to do that? If so, you're in good company. That's what happened to Jesus' disciples on the day of Pentecost. We'll hear about this miracle in a moment. But first I want to find out whether anyone here has ever witnessed a miracle, or has seen God do something amazing!

PairTalk: seen any miracles lately?

Ask the person sitting next to you:

> ▷ Have you ever witnessed a miracle?
> ▷ Have you seen God do something amazing?

Circulate as people write and talk, and see if you can find any amazing stories. Either summarise, or invite people to come up to the front and tell their story.

Watch it!

A moving story: Pentecost

This is taken from Acts 2.1–13, based on the CEV and The Message.

Divide the congregation into two. If you have arranged the chairs into a circle, designate an inner circle and outer circle.

If you have all the chairs facing the front, divide the congregation into front half and back half. The front half – or the inner circle – are going to be Jesus' followers.

The back half or outer circle can stand up, at a distance, holding a Bible. They are the religious Jews, 'from every country in the world' who were 'living in Jerusalem.'

Next, divide the 'Religious Jews' into two.

The 1's will later say: What does all this mean?

The other half, the 2's, will later say: They're drunk!

Choose someone to be Luke to narrate the bulk of this passage.

Choose a Jewish spokesperson.

The Leader needs to guide people on how to act at each point. Don't worry about having to break up the reading to do this. It will encourage everyone to listen carefully – and will be good fun!

LUKE: When the Feast of Pentecost came, they were all together in one place.

LEADER: Jesus' Followers, act as if you are praying.

LUKE: Without warning there was a sound like a strong wind, gale force – no one could tell where it came from. It filled the whole building.

LEADER: Jesus' Followers: you need to make the sound of wind!

LUKE: Then like a wildfire, the Holy Spirit spread through their ranks, and they saw what looked like fiery tongues moving in all directions. A tongue came and settled on each person there.

LEADER: Jesus' Followers: wave your hands above your heads like flames.

LUKE: The Holy Spirit took control of everyone, and they began speaking whatever languages the Spirit let them speak.

LEADER: Jesus' Followers: turn round and approach the religious Jews, and say 'Hello', using the language on their label.

LUKE: There were many religious Jews staying in Jerusalem just then, devout pilgrims from all the world.

LEADER: Jews, look very religious! Now move in closer and look surprised to hear 'Hello' in your own language.

LUKE: And when they heard this noise...

LEADER: Followers, let's have some more wind!

LUKE: ... they came on the run. They were thunderstruck, because they were hearing everything in their own language.

LEADER: Let's have some more 'Hellos' from Jesus' followers. Jews, you need to look amazed.

LUKE: They couldn't for the life of them figure out what was going on, and kept saying,

JEWISH SPOKESPERSON: Aren't these all Galileans? How come we're hearing them talk in our various mother tongues?
Parthians, Medes and Elamites;
Visitors from Mesopotamia, Judea, and Cappadocia,
Pontus and Asia, Phrygia and Pamphylia,
Egypt and the parts of Libya belonging to Cyrene;
People from Rome, both Jews and proselytes;
Even Cretans and Arabs.
They're speaking our languages, describing God's mighty works!

LUKE: Their heads were spinning; they couldn't make head or tail of any of it. They talked back and forth, confused. Some of them kept asking each other,

JEWS 1: What does all this mean?

LUKE: Others made fun of the Lord's followers and said:

JEWS 2: They're drunk!

Invite the congregation to sit.

The Shy Spies investigate: strange times in Jerusalem

LEADER: So were they drunk? What had happened that morning in Jerusalem? How do we find out? Time to call for the Shy Spies.

Enter the Shy Spies

X: I'm Agent X:

Y: I'm Agent Y.

X and Y: *(Together)* And we're the Shy Spies. Shhhhhhh.

X: We've come from our bosses...

Y: ...B and Q.

X and Y: *(Together)* And they've given us a mission to do. They want to know what's happening here.

First, they ask the religious Jews:
▷ It seems to be very noisy, what's going on?
▷ What was that huge whooshing sound?
▷ Are you followers of Jesus?
▷ What do you make of all this?

Next, they ask Jesus' followers:
▷ What this is all about?

Followers should be able to explain that they're followers of Jesus. They should tell the Shy Spies that what has happened, as promised by God, is that the Holy Spirit has come to equip them to witness to him. If X & Y need to, they should ask: Who is your leader?

The Leader of the service needs to take on the role of Peter. Then he can explain what was going on and tell them something about Jesus and his death and resurrection. (Summarise Acts 2.14–36.)

JEWISH SPOKESPERSON: Friends, what shall we do?

PETER: Turn back to God! Be baptised in the name of Jesus Christ, so that your sins will be forgiven. Then you will be given the Holy Spirit. This promise is for you and your children. It is for everyone our Lord God will choose, no matter where they live.

Shy Spies make notes or speak into mobile phone in loud whisper, reporting back

X: So we have a lot of languages,

Y: Three thousand people baptised,

X: A sermon.

Y: Miracles and wonders,

X: And the followers meeting together to pray and share their food and money.

Y: Everyone likes them, and each day their Lord is adding to the group others who are being saved.

X: Time to report back to B & Q.

They exit.

Try it!

Meditation: inside out

LEADER: Some of you have been taking the part of visiting Jews, religious men and women who perhaps only knew God at a distance. Some of you have been playing the part of Jesus' followers, who were there when God's Holy Spirit swept into the place and took hold of them in an incredible way.

I want you to think about how you felt about the part that you took.

Think...

If you were on the outside, did you like that? Was that where you wanted to be? Was it easier to watch other people receiving God's Spirit? Do you prefer to keep God at a distance? Maybe it would feel rather threatening to get too close.

DIY

▷How did you feel about the part that you took?

▷Did you feel like an outsider? What is God saying to you now?

▷If you were on the inside, is that where you wanted to be? What is God saying to you now?

What is God saying to you today? What do you want to say to him? Take time now to pray. Tell God what you really feel ... about being religious, about needing to change your ways, about welcoming his Spirit.

Think...

If you were on the inside, is that where you wanted to be? In the middle of the action? An exciting place, but a challenging place. A place where you can't miss the power of the encounter with an awesome God. A place where there is no holding back. He is in your face and you will have to get close. You can't avoid others, either. Because he will be telling you to tell others.

Is God speaking to you this morning? Take time now to pray and tell him how you feel ... about the power of the Spirit, about obedience, about living differently to people who don't follow Jesus.

Give people enough time to think things through and pray.

A moving response: Peter's sermon

This part requires some action from the congregation, so as well as having a Leader at the front, you will need at least one Action Leader for the congregation to copy.

There is no need to hurry this bit. It's supposed to be slow and reflective, allowing people the chance to respond to God.

If the seating is circular, you will need four Action Leaders, one for each quadrant of the circle.

If the seating is all facing the front of the church, you will need one Action Leader, raised and visible at the front of the church.

LEADER: As we respond together now, I'd like you to follow ... *(name of Action leader(s))*

When I say 'The people said,' I want you to say, 'What shall we do?' That's all. The rest will be fairly obvious!

LEADER: Let's stand to pray. I'd like to you to turn outward to face the walls of the church.

Congregation turn to the walls of the church, away from the Leader.

LEADER: God led the prophet Joel to say: When the last days come, I will give my Spirit to everyone.

God led the apostle Peter to say: Save yourselves from the evil of today's people!

The people said:

ACTION LEADER /CONGREGATION: What shall we do?

LEADER: Peter said, Turn round.

Action Leader/Congregation turns to face speaker.

Change your life.

Turn back to God.

Pause long enough for people to think about what this means

Be bold.

Action Leader/Congregation raise arms upwards

Be baptised.

Action Leader/Congregation swing arms downwards

In the name of Jesus Christ,

so that your sins will be forgiven.

Receive God's Spirit.

Action Leader/Congregation hold out hands as if to receive a present

---

Heavenly Father, grant that by your Holy Spirit

we may be washed clean and born again.

May we know your love in the new creation given us in Jesus Christ our Lord.

Action Leader/Congregation hold still in silence. Give them time to take this in.

Amen

International song

Here are some options:
  ▷ *Find a worship song in a different language to sing.*
  ▷ *Ask someone from another country to teach the congregation one of their songs.*
  ▷ *Find a song in another language in a song collection, e.g. Iona Publications, Songs of Fellowship, etc.*
  ▷ *Sing a simple song which uses Hebrew or Greek words such as 'Alleluia', 'Hosanna' or 'Amen', etc.*

Prayers for the nations

Let's pray for the nations we've been hearing about today

who were in Jerusalem at that very special festival:

  for Italy, Greece and Turkey,

  for Syria, Jordan and Israel,

  for Iraq, for Iran,

  for Saudi Arabia,

  for Egypt, and for Libya.

We pray that they will have the chance to hear about Jesus,

and the wonderful works of God, in their own languages.

We pray that God will pour out his Spirit on men and women who serve him,

  to prophesy and to preach,

  to translate and interpret,

  to persuade people to look for God's forgiveness.

We pray that many new followers of Jesus will be born,

will be baptised,

and will also welcome God's Spirit into their lives.

We pray today that thousands will sign up to God's kingdom,

and experience a revolution in their lives,

this day, as we celebrate the birthday of the Church.

Amen

Live it!

TakeAway: Pentecost postcard

LEADER: We're going to try a little bit of imagination now. Imagine you are in Jerusalem for the festival of Pentecost. Maybe you've come from Rome, maybe from Egypt, maybe you live in Jerusalem. And imagine that you were there, that morning, when the Holy Spirit descended.

What would you write on a postcard home?

1. Give everyone a blank postcard or some A6 size card.

2. Get the congregation to draw a picture on the front.

It could be

  ▷ *inspired by today's Bible reading*

  ▷ *the scene in Jerusalem on that day*

  ▷ *a picture of your church, inside or outside*

3. Write a brief message.

On the other side, ask them to write a brief message as if to a friend or family member or to someone they haven't seen for a while.

It could be done in role, as if Jesus' follower or a religious Jew, or written from their real selves, as at church on this morning.

Either way it should start,

Dear... Wish you were here!

People can decide to give or send their card to someone. If they are really going to give it to someone they know, it will become a completely different exercise! People will have to think about what they really are prepared to say about their faith to others.

Or you could decide to display them in church.

Gordon speaks pigeon

LEADER: Pentecost shows us that God wanted the Church to reach out – to speak in all different kinds of languages. Today Christians still learn many different kinds of languages in order to reach different groups of people.

GORDON: And birds...

LEADER: Sorry? Who said that?

GORDON: Birds as well.

LEADER: Gordon, is that you?

GORDON: Yes, and I'd like to say... *(makes a pigeon cooing noise)* That was 'Hello' in pigeon.

LEADER: Pigeon!

GORDON: Yes, I've been learning useful phrases in pigeon such as 'Don't sit there' and 'How dare you do that on my friend.'

LEADER: That doesn't sound very friendly.

GORDON: I'm not trying to be friendly. I'm trying to get rid of the blooming things. So I'm learning to say *(makes more pigeon-like noises)*.

LEADER: What does that mean?

GORDON: 'How would you like to be put in a pie?' So when you said about learning languages, I thought, 'I'm doing that! I'm learning pigeon so I can tell them just what I think of them.'

LEADER: Yes, but it's not quite the same thing, is it? I mean God didn't pour out all these languages because he wanted to tell people how bad they were! He wanted to tell them how much he loved them.

GORDON: I can't tell the pigeons that! I'll never get rid of them!

LEADER: That's why I hope some of us here will share our postcards with others. If Pentecost means anything, it means we should get out there and tell people what we know. It might be the first time they hear about it.

GORDON: It'll probably be the first time they've heard of Pentecost.

LEADER: What does that mean?

GORDON: Well, you should make more of a fuss about it, shouldn't you? It gets a bit forgotten with Easter and Christmas and all that. You know what I think – I think it needs its own food.

LEADER: Food?

GORDON: Easter's got Easter eggs, Christmas has got Christmas cake. Pentecost needs its own food. It's all about marketing.

LEADER: Well, what food would you suggest?

GORDON: How about Pentecost Pigeon Pie?

LEADER: That's quite enough from you, Gordon. But maybe he's right. Who can think of an appropriate food for Pentecost?

Maybe ask congregation for ideas.

LEADER: You know what I think it should have – a birthday cake.

Because it's the birthday of the Church. I mean, you think about it – before Pentecost they were just a group of followers, wondering what to do.

Pentecost was the day when the followers of Jesus received the power they needed to step outside the door and take the message to the people. That's the day the followers became a church. And the followers of Jesus have been the worldwide Church ever since.

Birthday celebrations

DIY

▷ Emphasise God wanted us to tell others that he loved them – in their own language.

▷ Talk about relative low profile of Pentecost.

▷ It should be celebrated more because it's the birthday of the Church.

You could do one or more of the following:

▷ *Make a birthday cake with candles (not two thousand!) Eat it later with tea or coffee.*

▷ *Sing Happy Birthday, perhaps in a different language*

▷ *Make a big birthday card*

▷ *Sing in the 'international' language that all Christians know, e.g. Alleluia, Hosanna, Amen, etc*

▷ *Give a present. It might be a donation to the church or the broader church denomination, or to a Christian organisation that works as an expression of the worldwide Church. You might give items that the Church needs for its mission, e.g. mugs, tea towels, soup, blankets. Or you could give money for overseas mission.*

Blessing

Outsiders and insiders, rejoice together!

People of all nations, celebrate God!

All colours and races, give hearty praise!

Jesus' kingdom is breaking through the earth and growing tree tall,

Tall enough for everyone everywhere to see and take hope!

Oh! May the God of green hope fill you up with joy, fill you up with peace,

so that your believing lives, filled with the life-giving energy of the Holy Spirit,

will brim over with hope!

Amen

(adapted from The Message, Romans 15.9–13, by Eugene Peterson)

Might come in handy

About Pentecost

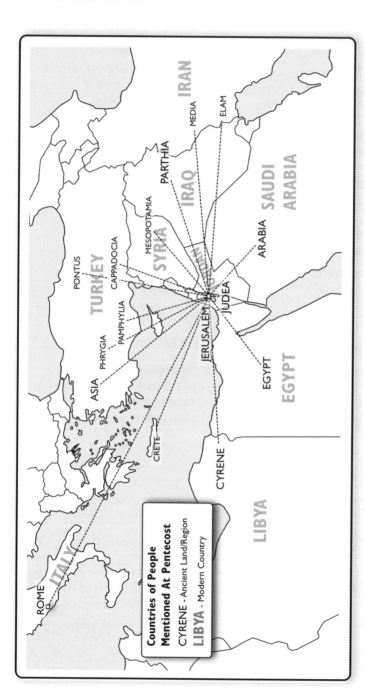

Countries of People
Mentioned At Pentecost

CYRENE - Ancient Land/Region
LIBYA - Modern Country

Pentecost is the Greek name for the Jewish Feast of Weeks (Deut. 16.10) or the Feast of the Harvest (Ex. 23.16). Originally, it marked the end of the grain harvest and took place on the fiftieth day after the Sabbath of the Passover week. By New Testament times the festival was associated with the giving of the law on Mount Sinai, which Jews believed took place fifty days after the escape from Egypt.

For more information about language groups and Bible translation, see: www.worldscriptures.org

Getting Ready

A week (or more) before

Questions

- [ ] Put questions on Power-point or notice sheet

Where in the world?

- [ ] Make or collect flags
- [ ] Write international greetings on labels

PairTalk

- [ ] Put discussion questions on Powerpoint or noticesheet

The Shy Spies investigate: strange times in Jerusalem

- [ ] Allocate part and brief actors
- [ ] Gather props/costumes
- [ ] Write/print off clues

International song

- [ ] Decide song

Comment

- [ ] Put map onto overhead display

Pentecost postcard

- [ ] Buy/make blank postcards
- [ ] Gather pens, coloured pens/pencils

Gordon speaks pigeon

- [ ] Copy script

Birthday celebrations

- [ ] Make cake
- [ ] Gather candles/matches

An hour (or more) before

- [ ] Arrange seating and set

Where in the world?

- [ ] Put up flags
- [ ] Make sure labels are ready at entrance

The Shy Spies investigate: strange times in Jerusalem

- [ ] Put props, costumes and clues in place

Pentecost postcard

- [ ] Put postcards and pens in place

Gordon speaks pigeon

- [ ] Set-up for Gordon (microphone, statue, etc. as required)

Birthday celebrations

- [ ] Prepare cake
- [ ] Make sure someone is ready to light it
- [ ] Prepare plates, etc.

Celebrations!

Harvest

6. HARVEST

Title: Use your loaf!
Aim: To acknowledge God as the Provider of all things
Bible: John 6.1–15

1. Want It!

The purpose here is to
▷ get people interested in bread and feeling hungry!

We do this by asking people to
▷ identify different kinds of bread or flours

The tools we use are
▷ Introduction: the best thing since flat bread

2. Watch It!

The purpose here is to
▷ hear how Jesus fed five thousand

We do this by asking people to
▷ listen to the Bible story
▷ listen to a monologue about the miracle
▷ look for clues about bread/ God's provision

The tools we use are
▷ Bible: John 6.1–15
▷ Drama: a NAFFF appeal
▷ The Shy Spies investigate: unbelievably fast food

3. Try It!

The purpose here is to
▷ understand how many people need bread
▷ work out how they could provide for the hungry

We do this by asking people to
▷ see the inequality of food distribution in the world
▷ discuss how they could feed fifty, five hundred or five thousand people

The tools we use are
▷ Comment: all the world's a loaf
▷ Discussion: do the maths
▷ Comment: who gives us our daily bread?

4. Live It!

The purpose here is to
▷ recognise God as Creator and Provider
▷ thank God for what they have

We do this by asking people to
▷ pray for those who are in need
▷ grow seeds
▷ listen to Gordon

The tools we use are
▷ Reading: the alternative Lord's prayer
▷ Prayer: Maker of the harvest
▷ TakeAway: seeds of hope
▷ Gordon's food
▷ Closing prayer

Running order

When	What	Who
	Want it!	
	Introduction: the best thing since flat bread	
	Watch it!	
	Bible: John 6.1–15	
	Drama: a NAFFF appeal	
	The Shy Spies investigate: unbelievably fast food	
	Try it!	
	Comment: all the world's a loaf	
	Discussion: do the maths	
	Comment: who gives us our daily bread?	
	Live it!	
	Reading: the alternative Lord's prayer	
	Prayer: Maker of the harvest	
	TakeAway: seeds of hope	
	Gordon's food	
	Closing prayer	

Want it!

Introduction: the best thing since flat bread

Hold up a loaf of bread. Invite people to come and smell it and taste it. If you want to go impressively large on this service, get together as many breadmakers as you can, and set them all to finish baking in the church just as the service begins. The church will be full of the smell of bread as people walk in. Sort of a post-modern incense thing going on there.

▷ Who likes freshly baked bread?
▷ What's your favourite thing to have with bread?
▷ What kind of food can you use bread with?

Bread facts

Use a few facts from the Bread facts (p.91). You could also put up pictures of bread from around the world. Try to get some pitta bread or naan, as this is closest to the flat bread of New Testament times.

The bread taste test

Have five or six different kinds of bread. Tell people what they are. Then get three volunteers from the congregation to come forward and do a blind tasting. They have to identify which bread they are tasting. Or they could identify different kinds of flour. Notice how they look and feel. Guess which kinds of crops are used.

Watch it!

LEADER: Bread is probably the one food eaten by people of every race, culture and religion. It's something basic to human life. As we shall see, the Bible talks about bread a lot. In the times of the Bible bread was a really important food, so important that even Jesus made it. Let's hear that story now.

Bible: John 6.1–15

Drama: a NAFFF appeal

This monologue can be read, as if someone is making a party political broadcast on the television. You can set up a large TV 'frame' made out of cardboard to enhance the effect.

SPOKESMAN: Hello. I am speaking to you today on behalf of the National Association of First-Century Fishermen and Farmers, or NAFFF as it's known for short.

Farmers are sometimes seen as people who don't like change. But here at NAFFF we have championed many modern farming methods. Given the shortage of water in this part of the world, we have led the way in irrigation. We are always irrigating. We are, perhaps, the most irrigating people on earth. And our call for increased mechanisation of the donkey has led to approval from everyone. Apart from the donkeys. Now they really don't like change. Anyway, we are not what you'd call stick in the mud. Well, sometimes we are stick-in-the-mud, but only when the irrigation system goes wrong.

And as for fishing, we have led the way in finding a solution to the most pressing problem that fishermen face – personal hygiene. We have instituted a system whereby fishermen negate the smell of fish by secreting about their person more pungent aromatics, such as herbs, garlic or onions. The result is our fishermen no longer smell fishy. Instead they smell largely of onion. And they tend to weep more often than they used to. Nevertheless, I am sure you agree these advances are a good thing.

However, it has come to our attention that certain members of our community here in Palestine are making a mockery of the work we are doing by producing meals out of thin air. We have it on good authority that, at a recent outdoor service, a well-known preacher and teacher suddenly and without warning, catered for five thousand people (not counting women and children) using just a few loaves and a couple of fish.

Now, I know what you're thinking: he must have cut the bread very thin. But no, it is more worrying than that. He apparently produced this in a miraculous fashion.

Needless to say, we at NAFFF cannot approve of this. This man has obviously no respect for the cycle of nature. And given the kind of conditions in which this food was consumed, he clearly has little respect for health and safety regulations.

Our members struggle against storms, drought, frost and the overwhelming smell of onions to bring you the harvest of the land and sea. They are hard-working professionals. Not magicians doing fancy party tricks. That's why we have launched the National Association of First-Century Fishermen and Farmers Opposition to Fantastic Food. Or NAFFFOFF for short.

There is an important principle at stake here. We are a nation who understand the way in which food is produced. All our religious festivals are, in fact, harvest festivals of different kinds. We understand that the food we eat comes ultimately from God and God alone. If a man goes around doing this, what does that say about him? Who does he think he is? He'll be controlling the weather next.

I look forward to your support. Please send your donations to NAFFFOFF, 3 The Old Olive Tree, Just behind the Gadarene Pig Farm, Galilee.

I thank you.

Try it!

LEADER: That's an amazing story, Jesus feeding thousands of people with a few loaves of flat bread and some fish. And although we talk about 'the feeding of the five thousand' actually it may have been more – the Bible just talks about five thousand men, it doesn't mention all the women and children! So how did he do it? Why did he do it? This is a job for the Shy Spies.

The Shy Spies investigate: unbelievably fast food

Enter the Shy Spies

X: I'm Agent X:

Y: I'm Agent Y.

X and Y: *(Together)* And we're the Shy Spies. Shhhhhhh.

X: We've come from our bosses...

Y: ...B and Q.

X and Y: *(Together)* And they've given us a mission to do.

X: We have to investigate this miracle.

Y: The one we just heard?

X: Yes. It's not quite right. There's something fishy about it.

Y: That'll be the fish.

X: No, I mean I smell a rat.

Y: Well, with all that food lying around...

X: No! We need to find out whether it's true!

Y: How could Jesus have done it?

X: We need to find out. And there's only one way! *(He produces his sonic clue-finder)* My clue-finder will find the clues hidden around the church.

Y: It won't, will it?

X: What do you mean?

Y: It never does. It's rubbish.

X: How dare you. This is state-of-the-art spy gadgetry. Here, I'll show you. *(As usual it does nothing.)* Oh. The batteries must be flat.

Y: *(To congregation)* Well, perhaps you could help us. Can you find the clues hidden round the church?

X: And remember – be quiet at all times.

The Shy Spies send the children and adults off to find the clues which have been hidden around the church. For each Bible verse returned they can be rewarded with breadsticks.

▷ *Clue 1: Psalm 104.14–15*

▷ *Clue 2: Exodus 16.11–15*

▷ *Clue 3: 1Kings 17.5–6*

▷ *Clue 4: Isaiah 58.6–7*

The Shy Spies investigate clue 1, which shows that God is the Provider of all things.

Clues 2 and 3 show that God has provided bread miraculously before – he's got a 'track record' in producing miraculous bread from nowhere.

Y: Jesus is sending out signals here.

X: He's speaking in code.

Y: Showing people that he's really God in disguise.

X: Well, that's solved it then. That's how the miracle was done. Let's get back and...

Y: Wait a minute. What about the other clue?

Read clue 4.

X: I can't make head or tail of that.

LEADER: Perhaps I can help.

X: Could you? Only we've got to report to our bosses B & Q.

Y: And then we're going to C.

LEADER: You're going sailing?

X: No – C! We're going to see C. He's the Head of Personnel. We've got to book our holiday.

They exit. LEADER reads clue 4 again.

DIY

▷ Send people off to find clues around the church

▷ Then bring out:

▷ God is the Provider of all things

▷ He provided miraculously in the Old Testament as well

▷ He wants us to share our bread with others

? ▷ What's it about?

LEADER: So, we've seen that God is the Provider of our food. And more, that we should provide it for others. Let's find out why we should share our bread.

Comment: all the world's a loaf

1. Divide the congregation into three groups

▷ The wealthy (17% of your congregation)

▷ the OK (25% of your congregation)

▷ the poor (57% of your congregation)

So, in a congregation of 25, you would have four in the wealthy group, six in the OK group and fifteen in the poor group. You can use the box to the right to help calculate the right numbers.

Total	Rich	OK	Poor
25	4	6	15
50	8	12	30
75	12	18	45
100	17	26	57

2. Divide a loaf of bread into the following percentages:

▷ 80% goes to the wealthy

▷ 17% goes to the OK

▷ The rest (and there won't be much of it) goes to the poor.

Obviously it's best to do the preparation before hand. Precut your loaf accordingly. A large round harvest loaf could be cut up like a pie chart, or you could use a baguette, ready cut into chunks – just count out the relevant amount

3. Explain that the three groups represent three different kinds of country.

▷ The rich group are countries like the UK, USA and Japan

▷ The OK group are countries like Poland and Thailand and East European countries

▷ The poor group are countries like Ethiopia and Bangladesh

The amount of bread they have represents the amount of food the countries have to share between all their people.

4. Within the three main groups, create smaller groups to discuss the following:

▷ How do you feel about what you've been given?
▷ How would you sort this situation out?
▷ What does God think about this situation?

LEADER: There are many reasons why this situation exists. Climate conditions, debt, corrupt governments, lack of education, war, famine, overpopulation and just plain greed all contribute to this imbalance. But the fact remains that there is enough in this world to feed everyone – we don't need miracles like the loaves and the fish. We just need fairness and justice and the recognition that it's not our food, its God's.

Discussion: do the maths

LEADER: So something needs to be done. We need to think of ways in which we can feed the hungry just like Jesus did.

Get feedback and, if possible, find suggestions of how this could be put into practice. Reinforce Isaiah 58.6–7.

▷ Assume that one loaf feeds five people and costs £1
▷ How many loaves would we need to feed
   a) 50 b)500 c)5000 people?
▷ In each case, how much money would it cost?
▷ If everyone in the church today gave £1, how many loaves could you buy? How many people could you feed?

Live it!

Comment: who gives us our daily bread?

LEADER: All Jesus' miracles said something about who he was. In the miracle we've heard about, he provided for people just as God provides for people every day. Although we often ask God to 'Give us each day our daily bread', we tend to think that food comes from elsewhere.

Reading: alternative Lord's Prayer

Perhaps a group of two or three could read it as if they were standing and participating in the liturgy.

Our Tescos,

Which art in the High Street

Hallowed be thy aisles.

Your kingdom come, your tills be rung,

On earth and online.

Give us today our sliced bread,

And lead us not into the confectionery aisle,

And give us our points, as we give you our money.

For yours is the Kingsmill, the Flour and the Croissant,

Forever and ever,

Amen

Get some feedback on what's wrong with this version. Then pray the real prayer.

Prayer: Maker of the harvest

LEADER: Lord, who makes the harvest;

ALL: We all share this earth, and we all rely on you.

LEADER: We pray for the farmer and the fisherman; for all those who work to provide us with food, wherever in the world they are. Help us to treat them fairly.

ALL: For we all share this earth, and we all rely on you.

LEADER: We pray for our fields and our forests; for the world in which we live. Help us to treat it with respect.

ALL: For we all share this earth, and we all rely on you.

LEADER: We pray for those who are hungry; for the homeless, the thirsty, the refugee. From all that you have given us, help us give to them.

ALL: For we all share this earth, and we all rely on you.

LEADER: Lord, you have given us so much; air, sun, rain, soil and seed. Help us never to forget who is the Giver of these things. Lord, who makes the harvest;

ALL: We all share this earth, and we all rely on you.

Amen

TakeAway: seeds of hope

Have cress seeds to give people.

DIY

▷ Remind people that God provides sun and rain to make things grow
▷ Give out seeds and instruction on growing
▷ Use seeds as a trigger for prayers or action

LEADER: God provides the sun, God provides the rain, God makes things grow.

To remind you of that, I'd like to give you some seeds.

Take these home and put these on some wet paper towels and give them some light. Then watch them grow.

As they grow, use them to remind you of what we've learnt.

Thank God that he makes all things grow. Thank God for providing you with food.

And maybe as the seeds are growing, you could use them as a reminder of something that you could do for those in the world who do not have enough to eat.

Gordon's food

GORDON: Excuse me!

LEADER: Hello? Who's that? Gordon, is that you?

GORDON: I would just like to say something.

LEADER: What's that?

GORDON: Man does not live by bread alone. That's in the Bible, you know.

LEADER: Right, well thank you for contributing.

GORDON: No, I just wanted to say, it's not all about food, is it?

LEADER: Gordon, it's a harvest festival. Of course it's about food.

GORDON: I don't mean that. I mean that Bible reading and all that. That story about Jesus and the sardine sandwiches.

LEADER: You mean the loaves and the fish.

GORDON: Exactly. You humans, you think that food is all that matters sometimes.

LEADER: Well, it's all right for you, you're made of stone, you don't eat.

GORDON: Ah, well, that's where you're wrong. We do like some food.

LEADER: Like what?

GORDON: Rock buns.

LEADER: Thank you.

GORDON: Gravel chips.

LEADER: Anyway as I was...

GORDON: (Interrupting again) Lava bread.

LEADER: Yes, well, anyway, back to your point!

GORDON: Well, Jesus talked about bread a lot, didn't he? And he said we should eat bread and remember him.

LEADER: That's right.

GORDON: And he said he was the bread of life as well.

LEADER: You're right Gordon, he did. We don't just need him for food, we need him for everything.

GORDON: That's my point. You said at the beginning that everyone in the world eats bread. But if Jesus said he was the bread of life...

LEADER: Everyone needs Jesus! Thank you Gordon, that's very helpful. (To congregation) So, what have we learnt? We've learnt that the food we have is provided by God. We've learned that we should share it . And we've learnt that just as we need bread, we all need Jesus.

DIY

▷ Jesus talked about bread a lot
▷ Jesus ate a lot of bread and used it as a symbol
▷ Jesus was the bread of life himself
▷ We need Jesus just like we need bread to eat
▷ Summarise service

Closing prayer

God of the harvest,

Grow in us.

Sow us with faith,

Water us with love,

Warm us with wisdom,

And harvest in us the fruits of the Spirit.

Help us as we live to go against the grain,

So that we feed and sustain others,

By giving, sharing, and loving,

Because that is what you have done for us.

Amen

As people leave, give them hunks of fresh bread to eat.

Might come in handy

About bread

Early Egyptian writings recommended that mothers should send their children to school with plenty of bread and beer for their lunch!

Bread and religion have a long history together. Hot cross buns commemorate Lent and Good Friday, Greek Easter breads are set with eggs dyed red to denote the blood of Christ, and Jewish families celebrate the coming of the Sabbath on Friday evening with challah, a light, airy yeast bread made of six long strands of dough which are braided to form one large loaf.

The record for producing bread from scratch is held by bakers from Wheat Montana Farms and Bakery. They harvested and milled wheat from the field and then mixed, scaled, shaped and baked a loaf in exactly eight minutes, thirteen seconds.

Scandinavian traditions hold that if a boy and girl eat from the same loaf, they are bound to fall in love.

About bread in the Bible

If the bread was to be leavened, then a piece of dough from the previous day (the 'leaven') was mixed in with the new dough. The dough was then left in a warm place until the yeast had worked through the whole lump (Mt. 13.33; Gal. 5.9).

In Bible times, bread was cooked on flat stones that had been heated. Or it could be cooked on an upturned earthernware dish placed over the fire. It resembled flat breads we have today like naan or pitta.

Bread ovens, where the fire was separated from the main oven, were not used until Roman times. These made it possible to cook thicker loaves.

Getting Ready

A week (or more) before

Questions

☐ Put questions on Power-point or notice sheet

Best thing since flat bread

☐ Organise breadmakers if you're using them

Bread test

☐ Source different types of flour/bread

A NAFFF appeal

☐ Cast monologue and ensure rehearsal

Shy Spies

☐ Photocopy/print clues
☐ Cast Shy Spies and brief them

All the world's a loaf

☐ Get baguettes/bread for the demonstration

Seeds of hope

☐ Get cress seeds

Gordon's food

☐ Photocopy sheet

An hour (or more) before

☐ Arrange seating and set

Best thing since flat bread

☐ Set breadmakers to make bread by the beginning of the service
☐ Set up plates with different breads/flour

Shy Spies

☐ Hide clues round the church

All the world's a loaf

☐ Cut bread into right percentages for the demonstration

Seeds of hope

☐ Arrange for distribution of seeds

Gordon's food

☐ Set-up for Gordon (microphone, statue, etc. as required)

Celebrations!

Advent

7. ADVENT

Title: I must be dreaming!
Aim: To show Joseph's faith and help people hear from God.
Bible: Matthew 1.18–2.23

1. Want It!

The purpose here is to
▷ make people want to find out about Joseph
▷ talk about whether God has ever spoken to them in dreams

We do this by asking people to
▷ tell us what they know about Joseph
▷ discuss dreams in small groups

The tools we use are
▷ Introduction: I must be dreaming!
▷ PairTalk: in your dreams

2. Watch It!

The purpose here is to
▷ notice how Joseph responded to God

We do this by asking people to
▷ watch the story being told
▷ move around the church
▷ repeat a chanted refrain

The tools we use are
▷ A moving story: Joseph's adventure
▷ Bible: Matthew 1 and 2
▷ Beat it: a chanted refrain taken from 1 Corinthians 16.13

3. Try It!

The purpose here is to
▷ listen to God

We do this by asking people to
▷ pray for those who need help making a decision
▷ pray for people around the world

The tools we use are
▷ Prayers for guidance

4. Live It!

The purpose here is to
▷ help people create a night-time prayer

We do this by asking people to
▷ write a prayer to say each night before sleep

The tools we use are
▷ Gordon's goodnight
▷ TakeAway: a prayer before bedtime
▷ Help yourself: dream on!
▷ Closing prayer

Running order

When	What	Who
	Want it!	
	Introduction: I must be dreaming!	
	PairTalk: in your dreams	
	Watch it!	
	A moving story: Joseph's adventure (including Bible readings and chanted refrain)	
	Try it!	
	Prayers for guidance	
	Live it!	
	Gordon's goodnight	
	TakeAway: a prayer before bedtime	
	Help yourself: dream on!	
	Closing prayer	

Want it!

Introduction: I must be dreaming!

LEADER: Do you want to hear God speak to you in a special way? Do you want to be a person of faith, brave, and taking risks, leaning on God? Then listen to the story of Joseph. Joseph is the hidden hero of the Christmas story. We know that he was married to Mary, but what else do we know about him?

One thing you might not know about Joseph is that, like his namesake in the Old Testament, he was a dreamer! Today we will look at his dreams and the journey he had to take.

DIY

▷Welcome and introduction

▷Ask how much people know about Joseph

▷Introduce discussion of dreams

?   ▷ What do you know about Joseph?

PairTalk: in your dreams

LEADER: But what about your dreams?

?
▷ How did you sleep last night?
▷ Did you dream? What about?
▷ Do you usually remember your dreams?
▷ Have you ever acted upon a dream? What happened? Do you think it was God speaking to you?

Feedback some of the answers.

LEADER: Dreams can inspire us and maybe even tell us things. Joseph's dreams did that and we're going to look at four dreams that he had.

Watch it!

A moving story: Joseph's adventure

1. You will need to identify three locations in the church to represent Nazareth, Bethlehem and Egypt.

2. You will need to teach people the following refrain taken from 1 Corinthians 16.13. Get the people clapping a steady four beat rhythm (4/4 time). The refrain is said over five bars of four beats (i.e. a twenty bar rhythm).

LEADER: Keep alert. *(2 beats: 1–2)*

ECHO: Keep alert. *(2 beats: 3–4)*

LEADER: Firm in your faith. *(2 beats: 1–2)*

ECHO: Firm in your faith. *(2 beats: 3–4)*

LEADER: Be brave and strong. *(2 beats: 1–2)*

ECHO: Brave and strong. *(2 beats: 3–4)*

LEADER: Show love in all you do *(4 beats: 1 bar)*

ECHO: Show love in all you do. *(4 beats: 1 bar)*

Depending on the size of the congregation you can do the activity in three possible ways. As the story is told, either:

> ▷ *the storyteller is the only person to move between the locations.*

> ▷ *the storyteller and a small number of actors move between the locations.*

> ▷ *the whole church moves around, promenade-style, with the story-teller(s).*

Each part of the story is around three minutes long. In recapping the story you might want to bring in the facts from the 'Might come in handy' section (see p.102).

Dream 1: 'Marry Mary' (Mt. 1.18–24)

The story starts in Nazareth.

STORYTELLER: Joseph has a problem
   Doing in his head,
   His girlfriend Mary's pregnant,
   They haven't even wed!
   And then one night he has a dream
   Lying on his bed...

Read: Matthew 1.18–24. Recap the story together.

LEADER: So, Joseph's first dream was that he should marry Mary. And we learn something else about Joseph here – we learn that he was a good man who didn't want to shame Mary. He was prepared to lose face. He was prepared to be brave and stick by Mary.

(Pray) Lord, help us to be brave and stick by our friends at all times.

LEADER: So they got married and then they had to travel. And where did they go? To Bethlehem!

Chant the refrain and move to the 'Bethlehem' location.

Dream 2: 'Go to Egypt' (Mt. 2.13–15)

At Bethlehem.

STORYTELLER: Joseph has a problem
    Doing in his head,
    He has a little baby boy,
    But Herod wants him dead!
    Then he has a dream one night
    Lying on his bed...

Read: Matthew 2.13–15 and recap the story as before.

LEADER: So, Joseph heard from God again. And this time it's another tough message – they must leave their home country and become refugees, running away. They have to leave what security they had and go to Egypt.

But Joseph was a brave man. He showed courage in leading and protecting his family.

(Pray) Dear Lord, Help us to be brave and protect our families.

Refrain

Dream 3: 'Go to Israel' (Mt. 2.19–21)

In Egypt

STORYTELLER: Joseph has a problem
    Doing in his head,
    He can't go back to Israel,
    Until the old King's dead!
    Then he has a dream one night
    Lying on his bed...

Read Matthew 2.19–21 and recap.

LEADER: So they're in Egypt, waiting to get back. By then, Jesus may have been as much as four years old, so Joseph must have been very patient in the meantime. He has to learn to wait until God's timing was right. Then he has a dream saying that the old king is dead. So it's back to Israel, probably to Bethlehem.

(Pray) Lord, help us to be patient and to wait for what you have to say.

Refrain

Dream 4: 'Go to Nazareth' (Mt. 2.22–23)

In Bethlehem

STORYTELLER: Joseph has a problem
  Doing in his head,
  The new King's just as nasty,
  Joseph's filled with dread!
  Then he has a dream one night
  Lying on his bed...

Read Matthew 2.22–23 and recap.

LEADER: Back in Israel, Joseph hears that the new ruler of the region is Archelaus – one of Herod's sons, and just as nasty and vicious as his Dad was. So Joseph is afraid to go there.

Instead God tells him to go back to Nazareth. Which is a bit odd. Instead of being brought up in Bethlehem, the town where the great King David was born, a town with a long history and big significance, Jesus is going to be brought up in Nazareth, a tiny town in Galilee – a region that everyone looks down on. God's Son, brought up in the middle of nowhere.

But Joseph was prepared to trust God's choice. It was not the way anyone else would have done it, but it was the way in which God wanted it done.

(Pray) Lord, help us to do what you want and trust your choices for us.

Refrain

Try it!

LEADER: So we've learnt a lot about Joseph. We've learnt that he was brave, that he was patient, that he was a good man and that he trusted God. He listened to God – even in his sleep! Are you facing a difficult decision? I don't want you to go to sleep right now! But let's take the opportunity to be silent for a moment and listen to God.

Prayers for guidance

This is a chance to pray for anyone facing a difficult dilemma or decision.

When people are silent you could ask those who are facing a difficult decision to raise a hand – they don't have to tell everyone about it, they just have to indicate that they are in that position.

Then you could invite people around them to place a hand on their shoulders and pray silently for those people – again, without being given all the details. Children can do this for adults as well as other way round.

Give people the option of talking or praying with others about whatever they are facing, either within the service or at the end.

You could provide a suggested prayer (e.g. in the notice sheet) with gaps for people to use, either praying silently or out loud.

Dear Lord,

We pray for people like Joseph

For people who are having to stick by others despite the shame

For people who want to do the right thing

For people who find themselves in danger and have to flee

For people who are living in exile, far from home

For people who need your guidance.

Be with them Lord, in their waking and sleeping,

Guide their steps, guard their lives,

And give them a place where they can be with you.

Amen

Live it!

Gordon's goodnight

LEADER: Joseph listened to God at night. I wonder what's your night-time routine? Do you pray before you go to bed? I hope you clean your teeth and all that stuff.

GORDON: I do!

LEADER: Gordon! Do you have a night-time routine?

GORDON: I do. Every night I clean the moss out of my ears. And looking at you, I think you could do worse than follow my example.

LEADER: Thank you. I'll bear it in mind. Then what do you do?

GORDON: I like to read a book.

LEADER: Do you? What are you reading at the moment?

GORDON: Well, we rocks like mysteries. Whodunnits. Anything by Agatha Crystal for example. But at the moment I'm reading a classic of Gargoyle literature. It's the story of an obsessive builder, seeking revenge on a great white stone that fell on his foot while he was building a church.

LEADER: What's it called?

GORDON: Moby Brick. And of course, I always pray at night.

LEADER: What do you pray?

GORDON: Oh, that God will protect me and keep my mortar strong and that if he's got anything to say to me, he'll let me know.

LEADER: That's a good idea.

GORDON: I think everyone should pray before going to sleep. I've got my own prayer written down.

LEADER: Could we hear it?

GORDON: Of course. *(Getting tired)* Only, just thinking about it makes me feel really sleepy.

LEADER: Gordon. tell us the prayer!

GORDON: It goes... *(snores loudly)*

LEADER: Gordon! Gordon! You can't go to sleep now... Oh he's gone. It looks like we'll have to make up our own bed time prayer. Let's write a prayer now that we could pray tonight before we go to sleep.

TakeAway: a prayer before bedtime

Give each person a card with the title 'A prayer before bedtime.' Working in pairs, get them to write down a simple prayer to pray before sleeping.

Help yourself: dream on!

LEADER: There are other things you can do to listen to God in your dreams. You might like to keep a journal of your dreams to see if God is saying anything to you. If you have troubling dreams, you might like to pray about them with your partner or a friend.

Maybe you could find prayers that other people have written to be said before sleeping.

Whatever the case, let us all try to listen to God. As Joseph's story shows, you never know when he's going to speak to you or what he's going to say.

DIY

▷Other things you can do to listen to your dreams

▷Find out other prayers for sleeping

▷Conclude Joseph's story

Closing prayer

Lord, as we go from here;

Speak to us, waking and sleeping;

Shield us from harm,

Show us your love,

Shape our thoughts,

And share with us your plans for our life,

as you did for your servant Joseph.

In your name we pray,

Amen

Might come in handy

About Joseph

We know that Joseph had family in Bethlehem, but it was probable that he also had a small piece of land there; which is why he had to return for the census (Lk. 2.4). Given that Herod ordered a slaughter of children under two, they could have stayed up to two years in Bethlehem.

It is not certain how long they remained in Egypt. Some early church writers believed that Jesus was two when he went to Egypt and four when he returned. Matthew doesn't tell us exactly where he returned to, but he was probably intending to return to Bethlehem – the town of David where it would be natural for the Messiah to grow up. However, Herod's son Archelaus had taken over and Joseph is warned to go to Nazareth instead.

About Herod and family

There is no independent historical record of Herod the Great's massacre of the innocents, but it is entirely in keeping with his character. Old, dying and increasingly paranoid, his final days were marked by a series of violent acts. He had his son, Antipater, executed. He had two rabbis burned alive; the death of some peasant children (probably only a dozen, because Bethlehem was small) would hardly have made the headlines. He made a late change in his will which divided his kingdom into three parts. Archelaus, who was notorious for his cruelty, was given Judea, Samaria and Idumea. So Joseph headed for Galilee

About Nazareth

Nazareth is some sixty-five miles north of Jerusalem. Unmentioned in the Old Testament, it was an obscure place, but it was not isolated – only a few miles away was Sepphoris, the largest city in Galilee. Nobody is sure how many people lived in Nazareth when Jesus lived there, but it was probably around four to six hundred people. People who came from this area were looked on with scorn by the more sophisticated people from the south. In Acts, when Christians are called 'Nazarenes' it's intended as an insult (Acts 24.5).

About Bethlehem

Bethlehem was only nine kilometres or five miles south of Jerusalem (see map on p.61). It was a place with rich biblical history; the native city of the house of King David, the place where Ruth came to live; the site of Rachel's tomb. The church there, over the traditional site of the birth, is probably the oldest original church building still in use.

Getting ready

A week (or more) before

Questions

☐ Put questions on Power-point or notice sheet

PairTalk: in your dreams

☐ Copy discussion questions onto paper or for over-head display. Copy visual prompts for discussion, if needed.

A moving story: Joseph's adventure

☐ Make signs, collect props
☐ Prime storyteller to learn story and refrain

Prayers for guidance

☐ Copy suggested prayer onto paper or overhead display

Gordon's goodnight

☐ Copy script

TakeAway: a prayer before bedtime

☐ Prepare night-time cards

An hour (or more) before

☐ Arrange seating and set

A moving story: Joseph's adventure

☐ Set up room to journey between three points: Naza-reth, Bethlehem, Egypt
☐ Hang up signs or props for each location

Gordon's goodnight

☐ Set-up for Gordon (microphone, statue, etc. as required)

TakeAway: a prayer before bedtime

☐ Put cards in place

Celebrations!

Christmas

8. CHRISTMAS

Title: The demanding present
Aim: To show how God's gift of Jesus demands a response
Bible: Luke 2.1–7

1. Want It!

The purpose here is to
▷ recognise that Christmas is a demanding time
▷ see what God demands of us

We do this by asking people to
▷ think about why they have come to church
▷ watch the drama
▷ discuss the demands of Christmas

The tools we use are
▷ Introduction: the Christmas pudding conundrum
▷ Drama: Junior's Christmas
▷ PairTalk: the demands of Christmas

2. Watch It!

The purpose here is to
▷ examine the real Christmas
▷ see how demanding it was and why Mary and Joseph were prepared to face the hardship

We do this by asking people to
▷ answer questions about Bible verses
▷ pray

The tools we use are
▷ The Shy Spies investigate: the unknown Christmas
▷ Bible reading Luke 2.1–7
▷ Bible verses: excited voices
▷ Prayer: still looking

3. Try It!

The purpose here is to
▷ offer a gift to Jesus

We do this by asking people to
▷ think about what they could give
▷ pray for others

The tools we use are
▷ Help yourself: offer a gift to Jesus
▷ Prayers: shepherds in the darkness
▷ Prayer: do it Lord!

4. Live It!

The purpose here is to
▷ see how Jesus had a demanding life and death

We do this by asking people to
▷ listen to the comment and the poem

The tools we use are
▷ Comment: Christmas in context
▷ Poem: the donkey's song
▷ Help yourself: get to know Jesus better
▷ Closing prayer

Running order

When	What	Who
	Want it!	
	Introduction. Christmas pudding co-nundrum	
	Drama: Junior's Christmas	
	PairTalk: the demands of Christmas	
	Watch it!	
	The Shy Spies investigate: the unknown Christmas (includes Bible reading Luke 2.1–7 and other Bible verses)	
	Prayer: still looking	
	Try it!	
	Help yourself: offer a gift to Jesus	
	Prayers: shepherds in the darkness – do it, Lord!	
	Live it!	
	Comment: Christmas in context	
	Poem: the donkey's song	
	TakeAway: get to know Jesus	
	Closing prayer	

Want it!

The Christmas pudding conundrum

LEADER: I don't know what your favourite part of Christmas is. Some people love the tree, some people love the presents, some people, believe it or not, love the sprouts. Maybe you love this.

Put a Christmas pudding on the table.

 ▷ Who likes Christmas pudding? *(Hand round small bits).*

LEADER: But I've got a question that is worrying me, a question which maybe you can help me answer: if Christmas pudding is so great, how come we only eat it once a year?

Feedback

LEADER: It's tradition. It's what you do. You've got to have a pudding, haven't you? Just like you've got to have a load of other things that you only use at this time of year – Christmas trees and Christmas crackers and bags of mixed nuts and dates and advocaat.

And maybe coming to a Christmas service is something you do just once a year.

So now you're here, you can relax.

Thank you for being here. well done for making it in amongst the many other demands that Christmas brings. You know what I mean, don't you...

DIY

▷Hand round Christmas pudding

▷If it's so great, why do we eat it only once a year?

▷Tradition – one of those things you do at Christmas

▷Maybe going to a Christmas service is like that?

▷Intro to drama

Drama: Junior's Christmas

Enter MOTHER, FATHER and JUNIOR with a pile of presents. Although JUNIOR is slurping from a baby's bottle, and wearing a baby's bonnet on his head, he should be played by an adult.

FATHER: Happy Christmas, Junior!

JUNIOR: We'll see about that. I wouldn't like to prejudge the issue.

FATHER: I thought this year we would do something different and unwrap our presents after lunch.

JUNIOR: *(Pause)* No. I don't think so. I think I want my presents now.

MOTHER: But why not wait a bit...

JUNIOR: *(Getting out filofax)* Look, I'm on a very tight schedule here. I need to have my presents open by 8.50 am at the latest if I'm to get in a few hours playing time before lunch. That way I can assess all the presents and work out which ones have to go back to Toys R Expensive tomorrow.

FATHER: Ah, yes, well, you see I thought we might do something different this morning. I thought we might go to church.

JUNIOR: I'm sorry? Church? Are you mad?

FATHER: Well, it is Christmas... The birth of Jesus. Carol singing. All that stuff.

JUNIOR: Father, I don't think you quite understand the position here. Christmas is about two things: presents and food. Anything else is not necessary for the enjoyment of the festival. Now, we are running out of time. Not only do I have all my presents to open and play with, but I have several satsumas and a large bag of mixed nuts to consume before lunch. Now, where are my presents?

FATHER brings out a few wrapped Christmas presents.

JUNIOR: Is that it? It's not exactly a towering pile, is it? Still, I suppose it will have to do.

JUNIOR opens his presents rapidly and without care, ripping off the paper. The first few presents are baby books, all of which he discards by throwing over his shoulder.

JUNIOR: *(Throwing book)* Rubbish. *(Throws another)* Read it. *(Throwing another)* I can't stand that author. His characters have no depth whatsoever. *(Opening another)* Hmmm. I might read that one if I can be bothered.

Finally JUNIOR unwraps a big present. It is a teddy bear.

JUNIOR: What do you call this?

MOTHER: It's a teddy bear.

JUNIOR: Thank you, David Attenborough. I asked for the 'Fluffy-Nite Deluxe Bear.'

MOTHER: That is a Fluffy-Nite bear – look, it says so on the label.

JUNIOR: This is the Standard model, not the Deluxe. The fur is of a generally lower quality and there is no interactive voice box. *(Starting to get angry)* This just won't do and I want it changed now.

FATHER: Junior...

JUNIOR: I mean, call this a decent present? A few tatty books and a sub-standard soft toy? I expect more out of you and if I don't get satisfaction right now, I'm going to throw a tantrum that will last until Boxing Day.

FATHER: Come on. Be reasonable. What about a bit of goodwill? Spirit of Christmas and all that.

JUNIOR: You really are out of touch, aren't you? I may be only two, but I know all about the spirit of Christmas. It comes in bottles and is labelled Bacardi Breezer. Christmas is about getting what I want. It's about my needs. Food, toys, drink – that's the spirit of Christmas.

MOTHER: *(Determined)* No. You're wrong.

JUNIOR: I'm sorry?

MOTHER: I've had enough of this. You're wrong. You're a spoilt little brat and it's time something was done about it.

JUNIOR: *(Threatening)* You are playing with fire, Mother. Have you forgotten my uncanny ability to wake the entire neighbourhood at two in the morning? Or what damage I can do with a plateful of pureed avocado?

MOTHER: You should be grateful for what you have.

JUNIOR: I would be grateful if I had got what I wanted. I cannot be grateful for this second-rate piece of tat. Get me a bigger present right now or I will be forced to throw up over the new furniture.

FATHER: All right, all right. *(Bringing out an enormous present)* I was holding this back, but now I think we'd better give it to you.

JUNIOR: That's more like it.

JUNIOR pulls the wrapping paper off. Inside is a big cardboard box. He pulls it over and looks inside.

JUNIOR: What's in it? It had better be good. Hang on – there's nothing in here! What's the point of giving me an empty box as a present?

FATHER: It's not for you. It's for us.

He takes the empty box and places it over JUNIOR. From inside comes muffled shouts.

FATHER: *(To MOTHER)* Happy Christmas, dear.

MOTHER: Happy Christmas.

Freeze.

PairTalk: the demands of Christmas

LEADER: Christmas can be a demanding time. I wonder what was the most demanding Christmas present you ever received? Maybe it was really difficult to operate, or tough to get out of the packaging. Maybe it meant you had to work hard – like an exercise bike. Or maybe it was a musical instrument which made a lot of noise.

> ▷ Have you ever received a demanding present?
> ▷ In what other ways is Christmas demanding?

Watch it!

The Shy Spies investigate: the unknown Christmas

LEADER: So Christmas can be demanding. And the first Christmas was demanding as well. Much more demanding than we think. To help us find out more, I think we're going to need the Shy Spies.

Enter the Shy Spies

X: I'm Agent X:

Y: I'm Agent Y.

X AND Y: *(Together)* And we're the Shy Spies. Shhhhhhh.

X: We've come from our bosses...

Y: ...B and Q.

X AND Y: *(Together)* And they've given us a mission to do.

X: We're investigating the Christmas story.

Y: And all I need do to find the facts is use my sonic clue-finder !

X: Oh, not that again! It never works, does it?

Y: I think you're forgetting something.

X: What?

Y: There's a first time for everything. Look. I press this button here and... *(as usual, nothing happens).* Oh. The MOT's run out. *(Producing a Christmas card)* Anyway, I've got this important piece of evidence – a photo from the scene.

X: That's a Christmas card.

Y: Yes, and look at it. It's a nice cosy stable; Jesus has a strange glow of light coming out from his head; Mary looks all serene and happy...

X: That's not evidence. That's what we think it was like. But the reality was very different. Let's hear some real evidence.

Bible: Luke 2.1–7

X: So we have a journey,

Y: An unmarried mother.

X: A census.

Y: A baby.

X: So why was it demanding?

Y: Do you have any ideas?

Get feedback from the audience. Use the Might come in handy information (see p.102, 122.)

The points you will want to bring out, either in replies from the congregation or spoken by the Shy Spies, are in the DIY box on the right.

Y: So, what have we found?

X: A young, unmarried girl finds herself pregnant...

Y: She and her husband travel seventy miles over difficult terrain...

X: She gives birth in difficult, cramped conditions...

Y: And the baby has to be laid in an animal's feeding trough.

X: They are visited by shepherds who were normally looked down on by society.

Y: That is one demanding experience.

Y: *(Looking at his Christmas card)* Somehow, this doesn't quite capture it.

X: Anyway, that's the story as it really is. And we have to ask 'Why'?

Y: Yes?

X: No, 'Why'?

Y: Yes, what is it?

X: I don't mean you.

Y: I know you don't! U's not here. He's off on holiday with Z and the other staff from accounts.

DIY

▷ Read the Bible passage, and retell the story, bringing out a different view of the Christmas story:

▷ Joseph went to Bethlehem because he was from David's family. He probably had some land there.

▷ Mary would have been the subject of gossip and scandal.

▷ Mary could have been as young as fourteen. It was usual for Jewish girls to marry young.

▷ The journey was long and demanding. It is seventy miles from Nazareth to Bethlehem.

▷ The baby was born in difficult circumstances. There probably wasn't an inn (See p.122) but the baby was put downstairs with the animals.

▷ The family were poor (see p.122).

▷ So it was not the fairy-tale picture that we are presented through Christmas cards and carols.

▷ Why were Mary and Joseph willing to go through with all this? Draw out the fact that the arrival of Jesus spelt freedom for people. Good news for those who had nothing (e.g. the shepherds).

X: No, I mean 'Why did this happen?' Why were Mary and Joseph willing to endure all this? What was so important about this gift, that they were willing to face up to all the demands?

Y: Well, that's for them to work out. (Indicates congregation)

X: There are some clues hidden around the room, disguised as Christmas presents. See if you can find them.

The clues are Christmas presents hidden around the room. Each has a Bible verse, either attached on the label or inside the present. Children and adults fetch presents and read the clues. You may not want to use all the characters or verses. Select the amount that you have time for. Together with the congregation, the Shy Spies work out why each character was excited.

Clue	Significance
Mary's joy: Luke 1.46–55	Good news for the poor and hungry; all generations will call her blessed.
Zechariah's vision: Luke 1.68–79	God has redeemed his people; his son [John] will prepare the way for the Lord.
The angels' song: Luke 2.10–11, 13,14	Good news of great joy; a Saviour has been born.
The shepherds' excitement: Luke 2.15, 20	Glorifying the Lord for all they had seen
The wise men's delight: Matthew 2.10,11	A new King has been born.
Simeon's welcome: Luke 2.25–32	I have seen salvation! Revelation for the Gentiles as well as Jews.
Anna's chatter: Luke 2.36-38	He is the redemption of Jerusalem.

LEADER: So we have seen that the birth of Jesus was demanding and tough, but that Mary and Joseph were willing to go through with it because they knew what it meant: freedom for all people.

Prayer: still looking

LEADER: Lord,

> there are still people living in Bethlehem,
>
> there are still shepherds and poor people who need your mercy in their lives,

ALL: All of us need you, help us to find you.

LEADER: Lord,

> there are still wise men looking for you,
>
> there are still kings and leaders who don't want you to take away their power,

ALL: All of us need you, help us to find you

LEADER: Lord,

> there are still mums having babies in difficult situations,
>
> there are still dads trying to protect their families from danger,

ALL: All of us need you, help us to find you.

LEADER: We're looking for you today, Lord

> everywhere we can think of,
>
> because we want to find you.

ALL: All of us need you, help us to find you.

Try it!

TakeAway: offer a gift to Jesus

LEADER: Christmas makes demands. It made demands on Mary and Joseph. And it makes demands on us today. What is God demanding of you this Christmas? Is there something he is asking you to do? Is there something he wants you to change?

The Wise Men responded to God's gift by bringing gifts. Is there a gift you can give to him? Maybe he's asking you to behave in a different way? Maybe you should put some of your Christmas money towards a Bible or a book about Jesus? Maybe you should give some of it away?

Here, there should be some silence for people to think and respond. Perhaps they could write a card to Jesus. Alternatively they could write their thoughts on a paper chain, which could then be hung up in the church.

LEADER: One of the things we can do is give the gift of prayer. We do this simply by praying for someone. Let's pray for people who are finding life very demanding now.

Prayer: shepherds in the darkness

Turn the lights down

Shepherds in the darkness:
Outcasts in the cold.
Help us, Lord, have mercy,
Help us share our gold.

Shepherds in the darkness:
Humble, poor, alone.
Help us, Lord, have mercy,
Help us share our home.

Shepherds in the darkness:
Tired and in despair,
Help us Lord, have mercy,
Help us Lord to care.

Shepherd of our darkness,
You have shared our plight,
Help us guard each other,
Guide us through the night.

Turn the lights up

Prayer: do it, Lord!

Lord, do what you promised:
Bring people hope and freedom,
Put humble people in places of power,
Give the hungry good things to eat,
Rescue them from their enemies
So they can serve you without fear.
Shine your love and kindness
Upon us like the sunrise.
Save your people from their sins.
Guide us all into a life of peace.

What, you can't do it without us?
Then, look, we've got willing hands.
We are your servants, Lord.
Do with us whatever you will –
For nothing is impossible with you!

Live it!

Comment: Christmas in context

LEADER: Mary and Joseph knew that when Jesus was born something special, something great, was happening.

They were also aware that Jesus' life was to bring even greater demands – Simeon hints at this when Jesus is presented to him in the Temple.

But in the excitement of Christmas we can sometimes forget the rest of the story.

And if we do that, we forget what Christmas is really about.

It's like having a calendar with only one day in it.

It's like having a great Christmas present and then putting it away in the box for the rest of the year.

It's like only having Christmas pudding once a year!

DIY

▷ People knew that something special was happening

▷ They were willing to put up with the difficulties because they saw how great the present was

▷ We only understand how great this gift was in the context of the rest of Jesus' life

▷ Jesus came to give us eternal life

▷ So Christmas is a cause for celebration

We need to see the birth of Jesus in the context of the rest of his life. Without the life and death and resurrection of Jesus, Christmas is just another birth, just another day in the year.

But it's not. Christmas matters because it brings us the gift of life. Christians believe that Jesus was born as one of us, lived as one of us, died as one of us and rose again, as one of us – all to show us the way to God. He came to bring us the best present of ALL: the gift of eternal life.

He himself said:

I have come so that they have life, and have it to the full.

When we discover what God's gift to us contains, then we have a real cause for celebration.

The following poem takes us forward to see what Jesus' life would hold.

Poem: the donkey's song

I was young when all of this started,
I was nothing much more than a foal;
I was purchased to carry this carpenter's wife
To sign the electoral roll.

It was some kind of administration,
The things that you humans do well.
We animals don't have to fill in no forms
We tend to rely on our smell.

His missus had been in a scandal,
Some people looked on her with hate.
I'm not rightly sure what had happened
But she hadn't half put on some weight.

I remember the time of the journey;
It was hard every step of the way.
And then, when we reached the end of the road
We found there was nowhere to stay.

This town it was packed to the rafters,
They were sleeping thirteen to a bed!
If they'd asked me I'd surely have told them,
You should always book up weeks ahead.

In the end we mucked in with the livestock,
At least it was somewhere to stay;
It was draughty and dirty and smelly
And I didn't think much of the hay,

But beggars can never be choosers
And soon things had got pretty wild.
And right there amidst all the muck and manure,
The missus gave birth to a child.

We animals knew he was special,
We didn't need to be told.
It wasn't the angels, it wasn't the star
Or the incense, or perfume, or gold:

It's just sometimes you know things are different,
Sometimes you know things are right.
And we knew there and then, what God promised to men
Had come true on that cold winter's night.

There were shepherds and angels and singing;
There were blokes with peculiar hats;
But the thing I recall was when Dad picked him up
And gave him a ride on my back.

Of course he was light as a feather
But I rocked him to sleep with each step
And they put him down in this old food trough
And he lay in my dinner and slept.

After that things got sort of, well, tricky;
They decided to set a new course.
They went on their way down to Egypt
And part-exchanged me for a horse.

Things gradually went back to normal
And people forgot what they'd seen,
Or maybe they didn't believe it,
Or saw it as some kind of dream.

But us donkeys we always remember
As sure as the day follows dawn
I'll remember the King of creation
Rode my back on the day he was born

Years went by and I moved to the city;
Well, the legs they were getting so slow.
I ended up working the graveyard,
Shifting bodies about, to and fro.

We'd instructions to pick up this villain;
Some weird, revolutionary guy,
So I pulled the cart right to the edge of the town,
To the place where they leave them to die.

And that was the next time I saw him;
He was frightened, and lonely and lost,
But the terrible thing was that they'd beaten him
And nailed him up to a cross.

Even though it was thirty years later,
I knew it was my little lad.
Oh, I knew it was him and I couldn't believe
He could've done anything bad.

He died not long after we got there
And his friends took him down from the cross ;
The sky had gone dark, it was raining,
As if nature was feeling the loss.

They tried to throw him in the wagon,
But I didn't want nothing of that.
I kicked and I yelled till they moved him
And I carried him home on my back.

He was heavier this time than last time,
With the weight of the pain and the years,
But I remembered the stable
And I remembered the tears;

And I remembered the baby,
As I carried the man through the gloom;
They lifted him off and carried him in,
And sealed him into the tomb.

Yes, us donkeys we always remember
And, as sure as the hairs on my hide,
I'll remember the King of creation
Rode my back on the day that he died.

But that wasn't the end of the story
Three days later and just before dawn,
Came this brilliant light, like there was on that night
Long ago, when the baby was born.

Now I kept my eyes and ears open;
I'd grazed near his grave night and day
And I nearly choked on my carrot
When the guards upped and scarpered away.

The stone had been moved from the doorway
And the graveclothes were down on the ground
And the whole place it felt sort of tingly
Full of noise; though there wasn't a sound.

It was soon after this that I saw him;
He was walking about bold as brass
And he came towards me and he held out his hand
And he fed me a mouthful of grass

He laughed as though nothing had happened,
But I knew things had changed there and then,
Cause the garden was singing like choirs
and creation had started again.

And he reached out and patted my muzzle
And I thought that I'd burst with pride
When he said to me, 'Mate, for old time's sake,
Once again would you give me a ride?'

Now us donkeys we always remember
And as sure as the ears on my head,
I'll remember the King of creation
Rode my back when he rose from the dead.

Help yourself: get to know Jesus better

LEADER: Maybe Jesus is just asking you to get to know him better. In which case, we'd like to give you a present.

It might be good for the church to have prepared a gift they could give non-Christians who are in the congregation who would like to read or think further about the demands of Jesus. It could be:

▷ *a copy of Luke's gospel.*

▷ *a booklet or a video or a DVD.*

▷ *a website designed to take people further into the life of Jesus.*

You could offer couples an evening meal with a chance to chat to each other and discuss things – a gift of peace and time to think!

LEADER: And we'd like to pray for you – and for all of us – now.

Closing prayer

Lord,

Christmastime comes with a splash, but the rest of the year we need your help just to keep our heads above water, to cope with the day-to-day demands of life.

Thank you for giving us a Saviour who rescues us from drowning and keeps us afloat.

Each day, give us

the joy of Mary

the vision of Zechariah

the song of the angels

the excitement of the shepherds

the delight of the wise men

the welcome of Simeon

and the enthusiasm of Anna.

Thank you today for filling us with good things.

You have not sent us away empty-handed,

You fill us with life.

Amen

Might come in handy

About Christmas

Christmas as a celebration is relatively recent. Well, I say 'relatively': it started in the fourth century. The early Church selected two dates on which to celebrate Christmas: December 25th and January 6th. These are the dates when it is still celebrated – in the west on December 25th and in the east on January 6th. Certainly the tradition from early times is for a conception in spring and a birth in midwinter.

About Mary

The mother of Jesus came from a poor family, judging from her delight about what the birth means for the poor. She was also probably quite young, since the usual age for a Jewish girl to be married was between thirteen and sixteen (although older marriages did occur). Parents usually arranged marriages through intermediaries. Betrothal was legally binding and could thus be dissolved only through death or divorce – hence Joseph's reluctance to do something as drastic as breaking off the engagement.

Jewish weddings usually lasted a week, with a lot of feasting among one's friends. The well-off were known to invite large numbers of guests – sometimes the entire village – to the wedding. They were joyous occasions; the fact that Mary didn't appear to get her wedding is just one more sacrifice she had to make.

About the 'inn'

The word which is usually translated as 'inn' can also mean 'guest room.' The Greek word Luke uses is *kataluma*, which also means guestroom. (In fact, the only other mention of an inn in Luke's gospel occurs in the story of the Good Samaritan – and there he uses a different word entirely: *pandocheion*. But he uses *kataluma* to describe the room where the last supper was held.) So the story of the hard-hearted innkeeper is an invention. In peasant homes of the time, the manger was inside the home, and the few animals that the family owned were kept downstairs. The likelihood is that Joseph and Mary were staying with family, but they were too poor to have anywhere to put them, except in with the animals.

About the shepherds

Shepherds were responsible for their sheep. Not only did they have to provide them with food and water, they had to protect them from wild animals or thieves. At night, sheep were often kept in simple enclosures made from tangled bushes, providing a minimum of protection from weather and enemies. Shepherds were poor, humble people, living out in harsh conditions.

See p.102 for more background on the Christmas story.

Getting ready

A week (or more) before

Questions

☐ Put questions on Power-point or notice sheet

Christmas pudding conundrum

☐ Get Christmas pudding

Junior's Christmas

☐ Copy scripts, allocate parts, rehearse

☐ Gather costumes/props

The Shy Spies investigate: the unknown Christmas

☐ Allocate parts, look at aim/scripts

☐ Gather costumes/props

☐ Wrap up clues (i.e. Bible verses) as Christmas gifts

Poem: the donkey's song

☐ Photocopy poem

☐ Find reader

Help yourself: offer a gift to Jesus

☐ Find enough cards or wrapping paper/ribbon/pens for everyone

TakeAway: a present

☐ Gather presents to give away, either gospels, booklets, videos, DVDs or your choice

An hour (or more) before

☐ Arrange seating and set

Christmas pudding conundrum

☐ Heat Christmas Pudding and cut into pieces

Junior's Christmas

☐ Ensure props and costumes are in place

The Shy Spies investigate: the unknown Christmas

☐ Hide clues round church

Help yourself: offer a gift to Jesus

☐ Put cards or wrapping paper/ribbon/pens in place

TakeAway: a present

☐ Put presents to give away at the back of the church

Appendix 1
Introducing the Shy Spies

The first time you use the Shy Spies you can introduce them with this dialogue.

LEADER: Hello.

X and Y: *(Together)* Shhhhh.

LEADER: Sorry. *(Keeping quieter)* Sorry. Who are you?

X: I'm Agent X.

Y: I'm Agent Y.

X and Y: *(Together)* And we're the Shy Spies. Shhhhhhh.

X: We've come from B and Q.

LEADER: Oh.

Y: Not 'O.' B and Q.

LEADER: Ah.

X: No, B and Q, not R.

LEADER: I see.

X: What have they got to do with this?

Y: I think there's been some misunderstanding. B and Q are our bosses at MI6–point-9.

X: That's MI6 plus VAT.

LEADER: Well, it's nice to meet you.

X: I'm not U. I'm X.

Y: And I'm Y.

X and Y: *(Together)* And we've got a mission to do. Shhhh.

Appendix 2
Introducing Gordon the Gargoyle

To be used the first time we meet Gordon.

LEADER: I'd like to introduce you to someone who's going to help out with these services. He's called Gordon. And he's a gargoyle. Hello? Hello? Gordon? Are you there?

GORDON: Of course I'm here. I'm always here.

Leader asks children if they can see where Gordon is. Get the little ones to say 'Hello' to him.

LEADER: So what are you Gordon?

GORDON: I'm a gargoyle.

LEADER: What's that?

GORDON: Well, it's kind of a statue. I'm considered decorative.

LEADER: Are you? Why? And how long have you been going to church?

GORDON: Six hundred years.

LEADER: Six hundred years!

GORDON: Well, when you're made of stone, time isn't the same. I'm considered a sprightly young thing. Graham Gargoyle over there is nine hundred years old.

LEADER: Anyway, it's nice to hear from you...

Then into rest of sketch.

The Gargoyle himself.